CONNECTED
GOLF

BRIDGING THE GAP BETWEEN
PRACTICE AND PERFORMANCE

JAYNE STOREY

AUTHOR OF *BREATHE GOLF*

CONNECTED GOLF

First published in 2022 by

Panoma Press Ltd
a Rethink Press company
www.rethinkpress.com
www.panomapress.com

Book layout by Neil Coe.

978-1-784529-66-6

"He loved to practice as much as he loved to play. That night in the ravine, he told me there was little difference anymore between the two activities; the pleasures of practice had become so profound. If I had stayed in Burningbush, I might have learned more about the 'second art of golf'... but I have salvaged some wisdom on the subject from Shiva's notes and some discoveries of my own."

Michael Murphy, Golf in the Kingdom

The Ensō circle is drawn by hand, often in a singular
brush-stroke that expresses a moment in time when
the mind withdraws and the body can move freely.

DEDICATION

For Mike,
my staunchest critic and greatest ally.

Thank you.

WHAT OTHERS ARE SAYING

"Jayne's work is a fantastic addition to building and improving people's golf games. As a former European tour player and now a coach, the fundamentals of centredness, balance, softness and stability that are so important to golf can be enhanced massively by Jayne. It is why Tai Chi and golf are such a good match! Jayne's work and knowledge are brilliant in helping people understand motion, balance and power. All massively important ingredients of a good golf swing."

Andrew Raitt, PGA

"Dear Jayne. Since starting with you, I played and won my first match today, beating my opponent by one hole with a birdie on the 18th! What it comes down to is that I simply do your drills and exercises to my best ability and then just let it happen on the course, trusting my mind and body together to work it out for me. That's the best way I can explain the seismic shift that I am experiencing. It really has been a shock to suddenly strike the ball such distance and to find I am on in regulation! You really have thought all this out very carefully, from the drills to the meditation, and they all work beautifully. Thank you."

Christopher S, Surrey

"Jayne's coaching gave me the missing link to pull my mind and technical ability together, and since then, I have had one win after another!"

Padge S. Winner, Senior NT Open, Darwin

"Jayne's teachings are the key to better golf."

Phil Scott PGA, Father of Adam Scott, former World No. 1 and winner of 31 professional tournaments

"I have loved working with Jayne on my breathing and becoming more aware of how my body is feeling on the golf course. I have come to the realisation that I don't need to interfere with what I am doing when I am in the zone; I don't need to start thinking or have a checklist of things I need to do like I have done in the past. When I am in the zone on the course, I can just let myself go and enjoy the moment, but when I do start to feel nervous or anxious over a shot, I now know a better way of helping me get back into the zone. When I feel nervous now, I just feel my breathing in the t'an tien and how my feet feel on the ground, and that helps me to get back to a calmer state where my mind and body can work together."

Gemma Dryburgh, LPGA and LET professional player, Women and Golf tour ambassador

"Training with Jayne helps me feel 'in the game' when I'm playing, everything feels right and I stop thinking about what could go wrong. I'm able to trust myself and commit to the shot."

Denise P. Winner, Swedish Junior Masters Invitational

"Dear Jayne, I was fascinated to learn more about how your Tai Chi methods and Mr Nicklaus' philosophy on the game have similar traits. Thank you again for introducing this new approach to us and for your creative thinking."

Andrew O'Brien, former V.P., Nicklaus Marketing and Communications

"My ultimate goal has always been to self-coach. I'm a very intuitive golfer and have never wanted to rely on lessons to teach me what I know is already in there. There is a type of wisdom in me that knows what to do. What blocks this very often is anxiety and overthinking, and Jayne's teachings have really helped me accept my swing and play some of my best golf."

Theresa W. Newport Beach, Florida

"Jayne, I really enjoyed your videos and your very low key way of sharing. For me, your information is spot-on and should be addressed with the pros as well as amateur golfers. Keep up what you are doing, and I look forward to working with you in the future."

Michael Hebron, PGA Hall of Fame

"I enjoyed your workshop and have begun practising the standing and sitting, pre-shot routine and set-up that you instructed us on. I played nine holes last Friday with no mechanical thought, only your swing feelings – focus on my navel, empty chest and rooted in my feet – and shot my best score of the year, for nine holes a 42. I only had three less than optimal swings, and even those were good misses!!! Clearing my mind, trusting my mechanics and feeling my feet throughout the swing made a big difference! Thank you."

Jay P. BACKtoGOLF Physical Therapist, Texas

"Just thought I'd let you know that my daily practice is going well. I'm getting a lovely feeling of power in your Tai Chi-style address position; drives getting out to 250 yards, irons going ridiculously far. Also, during two rounds over the weekend, I finally got properly into using my breathing as you've instructed and was delighted with the results – lovely feeling of release through the ball in the direction I wanted it to go – so thanks so much for this, it's a keeper!"

David Y, Rotterdam

"This is powerful stuff for those who commit to put in the practice!"

Jeff Hawkes, European Masters Champion

"Using her vast experience as a Tai Chi instructor, Jayne has developed an inventive golf-specific programme that will allow you to bridge that all-important gap between the driving range and taking your 'A' game to the first tee."

Mark Janes, PGA

"I had come to a perplexing crossroads in my golf and was very frustrated that I could not connect my athletic capacity from decades of traditional Karate and also softball into a fluid, athletic golf swing. Recently after listening to your podcasts and YouTube videos, I shot an 82 right out of the blue, with five pars in a row! Even after my goof-up hole, I parred the next. It was pure delight. As obvious as it should have been, I didn't think of attention and breathing as the way to go. I kept drilling positions and swing thoughts to see if I could make them 'instinctive' like my ball throwing or the instantaneous reaction of a Karate kick that flows from the nervous system with no interrupting thought. It is very inspiring to meet someone like you who has taken this fascinating performance conundrum, how to remove trying and thinking, and conveyed it into a practice for golf."

Ginny R. Portland, Oregon

"I recently had the pleasure of talking with Jayne Storey about her work with golfers. I was really excited about and interested in her concepts. Several days later, I competed in a Southern Ohio PGA tournament and decided to focus on her concept of being physically centred as I swung the club. The results were amazing, as I was able to hit 17 greens in regulation and shot an easy 69, a phenomenal ball-striking round for me! The feelings of balance, centredness and effortless power were great to experience. I can't wait to learn more from Jayne, as I'm sure she has discovered the secrets of peak performance golf."

Paul Hobart, USPGA, Founder of Golfers' World Summit

"Working away according to your instructions, I have noted a remarkable improvement in my ball-striking consistency. Secondly, much more enjoyment and less frustrations! I think I am getting into a new territory with a calmer mind, reproducible procedures, breathing well and rooted in my feet, swinging round that golf ball located in the t'an tien area."

Erik A, Oxfordshire

ACKNOWLEDGEMENTS

With grateful thanks to Andy Wild PGA teaching professional and Gemma Dryburgh LPGA and LET tour player, for demonstrating the various aspects of the golf set-up and swing.

Many thanks also to Alex Hiett for the illustrations.

CONTENTS

INTRODUCTION

Many years ago, when I was just setting out on my path, my mentor and friend who has overseen the writing of this book was a student with the same intense desire as me to understand what constitutes the perfect golf shot. We'd get together at the club where I was teaching and talk about everything he'd learned from years of taking lessons with swing coaches and those teaching the mental game, versus what I was trying to bring to the game from a lifetime of experience in the martial and Zen arts.

He shared with me the fact that in his search to understand how to play better golf, he'd been to several of the top coaches in the world and had asked them the same question he was asking me, but he found again and again that the answer proved elusive. Even though the elite coaches teach so many different and theoretically brilliant versions of swing theory, it didn't always translate into how a player performs on the course.

These conversations invariably turned to what my role was in all this, and I was asked many times to define my place in golf as I come from outside the industry and don't play the game. It was hard to explain back then because what I was teaching didn't tick any of the accepted boxes. When questioned as to whether I'm a swing coach or a mental game coach, I could only reply, "Neither."

It took many more years to define exactly what my contribution could be. Personally, I have now settled with being a Movement and Performance Coach, while the methodology I've developed (Chi Performance) has become the world's first Performance Practice: a simple, proven and trusted approach to help golfers and athletes from all sports perform under pressure.

This book confines itself to the long game while the learning is applied to putting in my audio programme *Connected Putting; Harmonising Mind, Breathing and Movement on the Greens*.

So, how did this all begin? In the late 1990s I became a Tai Chi instructor, having started learning this soft-style martial art in 1987. I was happily running classes at the local leisure centre, sports facility and social club when something interesting started to happen.

Having been incredibly shy and introverted as a child and young woman, it was only through my own dedication to Tai Chi as well as enjoying physical activities like cycling, running and going to the gym that I felt able to fulfil my potential. After several years of teaching, I became interested in working with sportspeople who I instinctively felt could reap the many rewards this ancient art had to offer.

Coincidentally, some of my students were interested in the benefits of their practice for performing better in the sports they loved, one of which was golf. So many of them told me that Tai Chi was helping with their competitive swimming, holiday skiing, recreational tennis and so forth, but, again and again, it was golf that seemed to be the most perfectly aligned with Tai Chi principles, so I began to investigate further.

My explorations led me to the game's greatest player, Jack Nicklaus, and I was astounded when I heard him say that "golf is played with the feet." This immediately struck a chord with me as Yang Cheng Fu − a famous Tai Chi Grandmaster − had said that 'Tai Chi is rooted in the feet', and this sparked a two-decade-long exploration of the many similarities between these disciplines. I had also been profoundly moved when watching Nicklaus' last professional appearance at St Andrew's in 2005, particularly when a BBC reporter thanked him 'on *behalf of millions*', as it was evident how important golf and sport are to humanity.

Since being inspired by Jack Nicklaus, I have dedicated myself to researching and applying the principles of Tai Chi to understand the fundamental laws of human motion, particularly in a performance setting. Helping athletes release movement that is natural and effortless in high-pressure situations has become my *raison d'être*, but as a one-woman band with 'different ideas', it's certainly been a struggle to bring my work to fruition.

However, I have persisted against the odds because there is an inherent truth about movement which has been touched upon time and again by players who have accessed the zone or flow. This 'other-worldly state' helps bring about a subtle relation between mind and body, thought and action, and renders even the most complex movement effortless and sublime.

Yet, in mainstream sports, the subtlety of flow which still exists in the performing arts like dance and music has been overridden by the insistence on coaching the mind and body separately. Golf, in particular, has become overly technical during the past few decades, forgetting perhaps that the early training of the game's legends like Hogan, Nicklaus and Mickey Wright, to name but a few, echoes that of the greatest warriors, including the legendary Samurai swordsman Miyamoto Musashi, who simply trained a state of *relaxed readiness* where intent and action naturally combined.

Even a cursory nod to the Eastern arts quite categorically proves that the quality of the practitioner's inner connection determines the quality of their movement, and my role is to help golfers activate this and thus enhance their performance and enjoyment levels.

Connected Golf brings you the authentic, centuries-old training that can activate the wisdom of the *bodymind*, wisdom you have surely felt in the moments when you hit the perfect shot and exclaimed, "Wow, is that really me playing?"

Berkshire, September 2021

PART ONE

CHAPTER ONE

THE EFFORTLESS SHOT

"Stillness is the master of motion."

Wang Xiang Zhai

According to a recent industry survey, the thrill of the effortless golf shot is the number one reason players give for their love of the game. It triumphs over every other aspect of being on the course and accounts for the thousands of hours spent practising on the driving range and the tens of millions spent each year on lessons and equipment by players of all ages and abilities.

The pull of the effortless shot is more alluring than any of golf's other treasures, including its social pleasures and camaraderie, the great outdoors and the obvious health benefits which we're now told can lengthen one's life by an estimated five years. It even triumphs over winning, which scored just 8%, placing it very near the last consideration the majority of golfers have for being on the course.

The pure strike of the golf ball is quite possibly sport's ultimate hook, even if it was a one-off shot that seemed to happen by magic some twenty years ago. It's what keeps players in the game, seeking and searching for this coveted yet elusive experience to reappear.

Curiously, it's something the social golfer, committed amateur and elite professional playing on the world stage can all experience. The perfectly connected shot knows no boundaries with regards to a player's performance level, handicap, age, gender, experience, number of years playing or even whether they've triumphed in competitions.

It can be experienced in the closing nine of a major championship, on a cold, damp Sunday morning at the local driving range or hitting into a net rigged-up in your garden. The thrill of hitting it pure touches and affects the spectators, even those watching on television, at least as much as it brings joy to the player. When we see and hear the pure strike, we know we are witnessing something sublime and astonishing that crosses all divides and it touches something deep within us.

When golfers contact me, I ask them to complete a short 'Player Profile' in which they can relay their game strengths and weaknesses and their most recent achievements, as well as what it is that they love about golf. More often than not, it's the satisfaction of hitting a spectacular shot, coupled with the wish to enjoy the experience again and again.

However, this is invariably combined with a deep disappointment experienced by searching for its secrets using the conventional routes of technical and mental game coaching, even though it may have previously manifested itself in their game.

Here's some feedback that has been gathered from those I've coached, including committed amateurs, junior players, golf coaches and tour professionals, and I've also added a few comments from the elite so you can clearly see that the pure shot is a phenomenon unto itself and does not distinguish a Nicklaus from a 'nobody'.

"I was tied for the lead and a little anxious about trying to capture my first tour win. I had 164 yards a little downwind, and I actually visualised the ball going into the hole before I struck the shot. I simply addressed the ball and trusted myself, and the shot came off just as I had seen it." – PGA Tour player

"Forgetting about technical thoughts allows me to flow better through my swing, and this encourages me to trust my ability." – PGA coach

"There were occasions when time would seem to stop, and I would be able to strike ball after ball without thinking about the mechanics of my swing. Unfortunately, I felt frustrated afterwards as I could not identify the technical details that allowed me to perform with such accuracy." – Amateur player

"Allowing the swing to happen instead of trying to make it happen is one of the great determining factors in how the shot

comes off. The result of allowing instead of adding muscle is always a beautiful, high arc, straight down the intended line." – Amateur player

"I took out my 5 hybrid, made a nice relaxed swing and watched my ball take off into the blue sky with a rather pretty draw flight matching the curve of the hole. As I watched it, I was a bit worried that the combination of draw and slope might carry it left into the fairway bunker, but to my pleasant surprise, the ball somehow continued to hang in the air long past where it would normally have dropped, carried well past the bunker, took the downhill slope and finished 30 yards short of the green. Needless to say, I spent the rest of the round trying to work out what I had done to produce such an amazing, almost out-of-body shot, but without success!" – Amateur player

"As for my greatest golf shot, I've had a few. The experience is the same each time. It feels effortless." – Amateur player

"Not only did I have a poor stance and have to stand closer to the ball than I wanted, but I also had an uphill shot of about 200 yards with big trees in front of me. It was a do-or-die shot, and I hit it perfect, wound up 18 feet from the hole, and made the birdie putt to shoot 69. I felt like I was looking at a bogey and somehow turned it into a three." – Former World No. 1

"Over the years, I have had about 20 deep zone experiences while playing and practising. During those times, which I remember vividly, I was completely relaxed mentally and physically, and I hit every shot exactly the way I wanted." – Amateur player

"One thing about perfect shots is that they are all memorable, and I remember the ball flight. A couple of them felt very easy, almost effortless, and the contact was pure." – Amateur player

Over the years, I've found it interesting that the word most people use to describe the perfect shot is *effortless*. It seems to happen by itself in a moment of sheer perfection. Balance, rhythm, timing, impact position and follow-through are all just right: easy but exact.

It's also interesting that nobody ever talks about technical thoughts or swing thoughts or thoughts of any kind, positive or otherwise, when relaying their experience of being quietly ready to commit to the shot, which always begins with a clear intention that allows the body to act accordingly.

In **Connected Golf**, I'm going to suggest and aim to prove that the perfect shot is the external manifestation of something that's taking place *within* the golfer; we might call this *the right internal conditions* where mind and body unite for the briefest of moments, summoning flow and with it the perfection of movement.

We can perhaps start to see the truth of this by acknowledging what every player knows about the pure strike, and that is, the more you chase after it, the further away it gets.

This brings us immediately to the first of three 'Performance Paradoxes', which I introduced in my previous book **Breathe Golf**. We'll be looking at each of these in detail in Chapter Five: Three Levels of Performance.

Briefly, Performance Paradox No. 1 states that 'The harder you try, the worse it gets' – and it shows up as soon as you get that taste of perfection. The tendency for most players is to want to experience it again, and they chase after it assuming it must have occurred either because their technique was spot-on or that positive self-talk over the ball is finally working.

Moments later, of course, when you've tried to repeat your swing exactly and sharpened up your inner dialogue, making just that little bit more effort to get it right, the next shot will most likely go awry, leading to the inevitable doubt, confusion, uncertainty and the ever-descending spiral out of golf and into that other game called 'Search for a Swing'. More of that later!

If we agree that the effortless shot is something like the 'perfect accident' as it generally takes the player by surprise and, when pressed, they will admit they don't know how it happened, then looking for answers using the mainstream approaches of thinking about your technique, swing positions and reframing your self-talk is looking in the wrong place.

It seems likely then that the effortless shot is not something to be achieved, in as much as we can't claim ownership of it. The origins of its occurrence seem to be in a realm beyond the mind and what our ordinary, everyday thinking and cognising can understand.

Moreover, the effortless shot is not something the golfer can muster through the usual channels held in high regard in golf and sport *per se*; the supposed traits that make up a champion's arsenal, things like mental toughness, determination, focus, brute force and so on, do nothing to encourage the perfect strike of the ball: in fact, they seem to produce counter results.

Maybe that is why it's called 'the zone' or flow, and golfers and other athletes who've had this experience often describe it as something otherworldly that comes from beyond themselves, something that just seems to happen.

When golfers try to recreate the perfectly connected shot using wrongly held assumptions, they make the wrong type of effort, forcing things, imposing their will, trying too hard and thinking too much. They come at it from the wrong place, just like the Zen archery master who tells his student, "You have too much wilful will; you think that what you do not do, does not get done."

I feel so many people have tried to write about this alternative paradigm which encompasses silence, stillness, the quiet mind, breathing, meditation and mindfulness, but without the actual experience gathered over many years of personal practice, the majority still approach it intellectually and present their *ideas* about it which are, for the most part, aligned to how they've succeeded in business and life generally.

Connected Golf offers something different; it's a methodology and 'Performance Practice' based on universal teachings on the mind-body connection and decades of personal training, exploration and research into understanding and applying these fundamental laws of human motion, particularly in a sports performance setting.

Helping athletes release movement that is natural and effortless in high-pressure situations has been my life's work, so this is not a general summation of performing under pressure but hones in on very specific training that allows your body the freedom to deliver the shot.

If you've experienced the joy of hitting it pure, you'll know that when you get out of your own way, amazing things are possible. Therefore it makes sense that you need to train to get out and stay out of your own way so that you can be influenced by something beyond ordinary thinking. This something is more joined-up and connected than the mind working alone, i.e. it's the intelligence of the *bodymind,* and you can't access this realm with psychology, neurolinguistic programming or by using models of the brain as a computer, all of which spring from the same level at which the problems of the mind are created.

As we explore the importance of the inner conditions of the golfer and you set about examining your own game from this different vantage point, you'll see that it's always the quality of your internal connection that determines the quality of your swing.

If we could put this on a spectrum, granted one that's forever changing and fluctuating, we might see that at the top end of the spectrum we enter the realm of Team Mind-Body (TMB) while at the lower end Control Freak Mind (CFM) dominates.

CFM can never produce fluid movement, no matter how much you know about golf technically or how much you might intellectually understand about the benefits of mindfulness, for instance. However, TMB can be accessed by various practices to produce the most fluid, powerful and precise shots you can ever experience.

What's on offer here is so clearly distinguishable from the majority of mainstream interventions that we could say it's a new, emerging world or paradigm of golf as a game of mind-body connection.

As our journey together unfolds, you'll be faced with a choice either to continue 'thinking about thinking' (mental game) and 'thinking about moving' (technical knowledge) or start training to bring these two aspects of your game together, which will allow your swing to manifest in the most natural way, appropriate to the situation.

The right internal conditions begin and end with establishing a link between the mind and body, and you'll learn ways that this can be accessed by anchoring the attention in the physical body, for instance, at the centre of gravity or in the balance point on the feet.

As you develop these Performance Practices day by day and week by week, your ability to allow TMB to appear as you stand over the ball can become stronger, and it needs to so you can overcome aeons of the preconditioned 'fight-flight-freeze' response in the nervous system. The training will also help you overcome the default tendency to start reworking your grip or your swing plane as the go-to response following a run of poor shots.

So, can I guarantee that by following this path you're going to experience the joy of more effortless golf shots?

Yes, provided you employ this new paradigm alongside your usual training, which, of course, I'm not suggesting you abandon; after all, swing coaching and sports psychology have their place in your development as a golfer, just not when you're playing golf!

All my research and the feedback from hundreds of students categorically shows that the perfect shot does not come either from the mind or the body working in isolation but from a union or marriage of them both.

The effortless shot is effortlessly connected physically when the mind and body are more related; the kinetic chain of events unfolds as a result of the golfer's *bodymind* being summoned in the moments before movement begins. This is in stark contrast to thinking about and trying to create things like tempo or spiral motion.

By priming the internal conditions which best allow the perfect shot to manifest itself, you can intuitively deliver your intent. Subduing the analytical mind, trusting first instincts and committing to the shot as a reaction to intention will revolutionise your game.

This is the essence of the book's message; inner connection leads to connected movement, and we're going to relate everything from the biochemistry of anxiety to the biomechanics of movement back to this one overriding theme.

I hope you enjoy the journey, and, just to be clear, the Performance Practices you're going to learn are not my methods but component parts of training systems that go back hundreds, even thousands of years. My part in all this is to help you slowly but surely build belief in this new paradigm while you need to agree to give it a chance.

Through the various TRY THIS exercises, you'll be asked to make a different kind of effort for your game, which will ultimately entail calling upon the higher intelligence of the mind-body connection. If you can do this, you'll soon start playing a game where you can finally trust yourself, have greater freedom of movement and release your own natural swing.

However, I'm jumping ahead of myself because the first thing to learn about the mind-body connection is that we don't have one, or rather, it's highly elusive, and like everything else to do with the performance of complex movement skills like the golf swing, it is paradoxical in nature.

CHAPTER TWO

THE INHERENT DISCONNECT

"Our body and mind are not two and not one. If you think your body and mind are two, that is wrong; if you think they are one, that is also wrong. Our body and mind are both two and one."

Shunryu Suzuki

Here's a question for you. Why is it that an elite golfer, as well as the committed amateur, can deliver fluid, powerful and precise shots on the driving range, or even early on in a tournament, and that during such times they can hit brilliant, even sublime shots, striking the ball just right whether for a power shot off the tee or a second shot from the fairway, but then as the pressure mounts their technique seems to fall apart?

Conventional wisdom and mainstream coaching will have you believe there are but two main reasons for this unhappy phenomenon which we see with alarming regularity in all sports, even at the world-class and Olympic level, and that these causes both reside in the athlete's mind.

In golf, it's believed by the majority of the industry that when a player's swing breaks down under pressure, either they have a blind spot in their technique, a position or plane that needs adjusting, or they're just not tough enough mentally. The interventions that seek to rectify and put right the wayward swing and negative thought processes are swing coaching and the mental game, respectively, and the various methods and differing approaches therein.

As spectators, when we watch an elite golfer's meltdown at one of the year's major championships, especially if they've gone into the Sunday with a lead of several shots only to squander it in an agonising and sometimes embarrassing way, everybody from television commentators and coaches to journalists will expound upon the two aforementioned causes (poor technique and lack of mental toughness) sometimes in excruciating detail.

They will demonstrate their belief in these causes by explaining that the player's technique has broken down because some minor or major point about their swing mechanics isn't right and needs fixing, perhaps by tweaking something in their grip or set-up posture. Or they will claim that the swing shape or plane wasn't right or that they need a complete overhaul with a new swing coach and a different approach.

They will also posit the notion that perhaps the player hasn't yet learned how to win or they don't have a high enough level of self-belief, and somehow all of these things affected their ability to swing the golf club well, even though it's likely that earlier on in the tournament, none of these faults were showing up.

The majority of players also buy into these myths because if everybody in the industry says it's a technical or mental game flaw, then it must be true, right? Yet even though players and spectators alike profess to believe this, my feeling is that they simultaneously know it isn't so, but how does one go against the power of such mass hypnosis?

When things go wrong, golfers seek to correct them using the orthodox approaches by opting for more swing tweaking, getting a stronger body at the gym and learning to 'tough it out' using motivational and achievement psychology. However, as we've seen, no sooner has a player in the modern age won a major championship than the next time they're in contention, especially if the expectation is for them to win, their swing breaks down, they miss the cut, and it's the same story all over again.

And what of the opposite scenario, when things go right, and everything just flows for the player when they're leading in a tournament? Again, the industry commentators and figureheads will explain it away by saying they had good technique, that they could trust their swing and believed they could win, but, as we've seen, when pressed about the experience of the effortless shot, everyone from weekend warrior to major champion tells a very different story indeed.

In Chapter One: The Effortless Shot, we started to explore the idea that it's the conditions *within* the golfer, in other words, their inner state, characterised by the quality of their mind-body connection, or lack of it, that ultimately determine the quality of their shot-making.

The subtlety of this is overridden in the modern game as intention and movement have become so divided due to the emphasis given to technical thoughts and the minutiae of various swing positions.

I'm not, of course, disparaging swing coaching, nor am I criticising mental game coaching, but what I *am* saying is that there's a place for these things, and, contrary to popular belief, it isn't on the golf course.

This situation with the modern game is nobody's fault; it's just the way things have unfolded alongside technological breakthroughs and the advent of the information age, but learning nothing other than technical and psychological interventions eventually becomes counterproductive to player development.

Deep down, I believe everybody knows this, but how do we break the mould?

So far, there hasn't really been a language, model or methodology to explain the phenomenon of the perfect shot, but it does seem to depend on where you are on the spectrum between TMB and CFM in the moments before you take the club away; the former manifests itself in a connected shot while the latter throws up your most common swing faults, no matter how much you know about swing positions or how long you've been playing the game.

In the mainstream approach to coaching, there are few words a player could use to describe or relay the subtlety of the TMB experience to their coach or when being interviewed by the press, other than perhaps to say that they felt comfortable over the ball or their swing came together, but without a workable methodology to help train this state, they are dangerously close to being caught in a trap.

We're going to examine these inner conditions more closely throughout the book but, for now, let's confine ourselves to saying that TMB is a unique quality of *relaxed readiness* so often seen in the demeanour of athletes from other more reactive sports like baseball or tennis, as well as exponents of the world's various martial arts styles.

The state of relaxed readiness is characterised by a calm and quiet mind, which is nevertheless still focused and concentrated in the moment; this brings about clarity of intention, which in turn activates the body to move the way it needs to.

Coupled with a relaxed yet athletic posture and strict adherence to some fundamental principles like being properly balanced and using the body's centre of gravity (all of which we're going to look at together), the golf swing can become a whole-body movement rather than a number of individual positions.

Moreover, when these conditions have been met, something like an *'inner set-up'* appears, which enables the player to intuitively deliver their intent; the doorway into the zone has opened, the mind and body seamlessly communicate because the analytical part of the mind has been subdued.

The result is effortless movement, and this shows up not just in the game of golf but in all sports and the performing arts like dance and music. In this state, which is just beyond our own capabilities, movement is rendered sublime, graceful and extraordinary like the ecstatic state of *duende* in flamenco, which takes the dancer, musicians and audience into another realm, beyond mere technical excellence.

As you'll discover, the Performance Practices within **Connected Golf** are the work needed to be granted access to this realm.

Once you start to look deeper at the laws governing human motion, especially in a high-pressure setting, you'll see that stillness and movement are two sides of the same coin, just like the mind and the body; neither must take precedence over the other but they must work together to form a unique condition which, although language can't do it justice, we might label as flow, the zone or the meditative state (Zen-mind).

It's my belief that this state is the natural birthright of every golfer (to wit: its appearance in both beginner and elite) although a special kind of effort is needed to summon it, one which is overridden by the tendency to try too hard and think too much, rather than inviting this inner condition to appear, which then allows movement to emerge naturally.

If we go back in history, many hundreds of years before swing technique, sports science and biomechanics were even thought of, we can use the martial and Zen arts of the East from archery to kung-fu and swordsmanship as our benchmark for exploring and summoning this inner state.

This is something we're going to examine much more closely in Part Two, particularly the condition of preparedness for a fist punch that is a unique combination of intention and action. Later on, you'll get to examine the similarities of a kung-fu punch with your own golf swing, but, for now, here's your first exercise in *Connected Golf*.

TRY THIS NO. 1
RECALLING YOUR FAVOURITE SHOT

Think for a few moments about your favourite shot of all time and try to recall your internal state in the moments *before* you swung the club. Chances are you experienced something like a state of 'relaxed readiness' with a quiet focus, clarity of intent and a commitment to motion without anxiety, mental interference or trying to 'get it right'.

Explore this in as much detail as you can, perhaps making some notes in a Training Journal, which will be useful as we work together. Please don't jot ideas down on your phone or tablet but use a pen and paper; all the research shows that writing in this way creates a better connection between mind and body, and as this is something you'll want to strengthen, now is a good time to start.

While swing coaching and the mental game remain important for player development off the course, i.e. when you are practising and honing your skills, the accepted approach of taking swing thoughts into the game, tweaking technique in the middle of a round and reframing self-talk so that your thoughts are positive and self-affirming, does little to ensure fluidity of movement. When emphasised too much, they are actually detrimental to the quality of your shot-making.

Together we're going to challenge conventional wisdom by drawing out your own experiences and laying the ground for a new paradigm in golf by demonstrating with research, anecdotes, student stories, feedback and supporting evidence that the problems arising in golf are neither technical nor mental but due to the actual separation of the *bodymind*.

That is the disconnection of the mental and physical aspects of the golfer, which begin with the way the game and sports performance per se is currently taught and practised.

In fact, we're starting from a place of disconnection, which then gets compounded by the emphasis put on swing positions and positive thinking without any attempt to bring them together.

Our inherent disconnection is that the mind, or more specifically our mental attention, is rarely, if ever, connected to the body. The mind is usually anywhere but where we are now, either ruminating on the past or projecting into the future, but rarely anchored in the present reality, whether that's the sensation of the physical body or the breath you are taking this moment.

This means that we are all led through life, and players are led through a round of golf, by the mind alone, a mind which wants to take over and tries to run the whole show just like a bullying CEO wants to micromanage their employees.

But is it really true that the mind and body are not connected? How can we know this?

Well, we usually have very little awareness of the physical body even though we're performing tasks with the body day and night like brushing our teeth, making a cup of coffee, texting, driving, washing-up and so forth, all of which require enormous physical dexterity but somehow we remain absent from the body and can do all of these things without paying the slightest bit of attention.

So what's the problem with this, if we can function physically without thinking about it?

Well, as we tend to live in the mind, we don't enjoy a joined-up or connected existence with the mind, body and emotions in harmony, but one that's piecemeal, one in which we are fragmented and where one part of us dominates, taking us away from the moment we're in.

How often have you driven home from work or to the golf club only to arrive at your destination without having paid any attention to the route?

The mind is so strong that you can *think about your swing* rather than experience the feeling of it. Similarly, you can think about tempo and think about ground pressure without having awareness of your own body's natural rhythm or feeling your feet supporting you.

When something is wrong with the body and we feel pain or discomfort, the mind and body are more related than they are ordinarily but not in any positive way. For instance, when we have earache or toothache or an ingrowing toenail all we can think about is how much it hurts, and we can't stop being aware of the part of our body that's causing us pain.

Then, when we're better, and the pain or discomfort subsides, we're no longer able to even remember we have a big toe or a left ear as the body merges into the background and our thoughts take over once again.

Yet it's the *body* that swings the golf club, and here's the essential dichotomy that we face in golf and sports performance generally.

The mind and the body have two different functions, two different jobs or roles to perform, even different speeds at which they operate. The mind cannot take over the role of the body and perform the functions of the physical body (although this is what the conventional approach to coaching requires), just as the body cannot take over the functions of the mind.

At best, the mind works in isolation from the body, which an elite player relying on technical excellence alone can get away with until the moment pressure comes into the equation. Then analysis takes over, the breath gets shallower, the stress-response kicks in and the mind starts interfering with the release of movement, rendering the swing out of sync, lacking rhythm, off-target and so forth.

The mind is meant to analyse, solve problems, organise, order, sort, quantify and understand information; that's its role, its job, its function – but it *cannot* influence movement except to hinder it and get in the way *unless* it can be brought into relationship with the body. This is the essential component of the inner set-up which brings a totally different, almost magical quality to the shot-making.

In contrast to the mind, the body is designed to process energy by way of the air we breathe and the food we eat and to move us through time and space for the duration of our lives. The body loves to move, and the proof of this is easy to see; for instance, how often have you felt tired or lethargic but gone out for a walk, run or bike ride and felt full of energy afterwards?

Moreover, the body loves responding to natural laws of motion like gravity, leverage and spin, which form the basis for so many sporting and athletic pursuits from kicking a ball, hitting a ball with a cue, club or racket, skiing down or climbing up the side of a mountain or diving into the water.

Later on, we'll look at how these natural forces work more efficiently when they are allowed to come *through* the body via an athletic yet relaxed structure, rather than when the mind tries to unnaturally force any component part of the kinetic chain.

You only have to picture an Aikido or Tai Chi master standing strong in their legs and moving around an invisible centre of gravity, sending their opponents flying using very little physical force, to get a glimpse of connected movement.

Understanding the internal conditions that give rise to this, we can deconstruct it, start to train for it and thus lay the groundwork for the spontaneous release of the perfect swing to show up in your game again and again.

Bringing mental attention to the sensation of the body and the breathing forms a major part of Eastern philosophy and practice and is not just about sitting on your cushion following your breathing, as important as this is, but expands into washing your food bowl and sweeping the dust off the temple steps. Every physical action is done with attention, coupled with the actual sensation of the body itself attending to the task.

The emphasis of such practices is to help us connect more fully to the present moment, to be where we are, and this profound notion is so extremely useful for golf, particularly as you're standing over the ball. The joined-up *bodymind* has an innate intelligence that needs nothing further from us than an attempt to bring our normally separated parts together. When mental and physical attention come together, and the mind stays connected to the sensation of the body, something very significant changes: we are calmer, more centred, relaxed yet focused, our senses are heightened, our balance is better, our movement freer.

Here's a lovely description of the spontaneous, almost accidental experience of such a moment by a new student, along with the sad admission that this elusive state has been difficult to recapture.

> *"I wanted to relate my most satisfying experience I had on the course. I finished work on a Friday and had no plans for the evening and decided to go to the course to practise. It was a beautiful night. On the practice range, a friend whom I had never played with asked me to play. He was a much better player, and I would never have asked him to play. We went out walking on the course and at 7.00 PM were the only people playing. I was relaxed with no expectations. I played the best golf, hitting all drives in the fairway and greens in regulation. With the sun setting, I saw the course in a different light, and it was fantastic. I also had an awareness of where my club was in space and no feelings of tension. I have not come close to replicating this again."*
>
> **Scott P.** Pittsburg, PA

Now let's listen to the feedback from another, more long-term student, who dedicated herself over several weeks to the various Performance Practices you're going to learn, resulting in what she describes as 'synced-up trust'.

"Hi Jayne,

I just had to follow up with you about how my golf felt today. I incorporated the right feeling in my swing with my feet today, as we explored yesterday in our Skype session. And it felt wonderful!!! All of my buddies really complimented me on my golf today, and especially one of the ladies I don't golf with too often. After the round, she said to me, 'I have to tell you, Theresa, it was really enjoyable golfing with you today. You just have such a nice rhythm and tempo. It was really neat to see that. I learned a lot from you today.' That was so nice to hear.

And even though it's not about the score for me... it's about that feeling of synced-up trust... I had a nice score today... so I just had to share with you... and thank you!!!

Much appreciated."

Theresa W. Newport Beach, CA

TRY THIS NO. 2
TRAINING THE MIND-BODY CONNECTION

In my book **Breathe Golf** I asked you to stay with your breathing while reading or listening to the audio; this time, I am going to ask you to stay with the sensation of your physical body and our simplest starting point can be the feet.

As you continue to read the next few paragraphs, aim to keep some of your attention on your right foot and the lower part of your right leg. You may feel this as the sensation of your foot and its connection to the ground or within your shoe. You will probably find that the mind's connection to and awareness of the body is so fleeting and that a special kind of effort is required to stay with it.

It's quite likely that you have already lost this connection as the thread of attention that connects mind and body is tenuous and rather fragile, and the moment the mind gets interested in something, even pondering on this very phenomenon, the physical sensation is lost, and we come out of sync and revert to being led by the mind without any connection to the body.

Try this exercise as often as you remember.

The opposite of 'synced-up trust', as Theresa has so beautifully described, is the inherent disconnection of mind from body, which in turn exacerbates the disconnection of movement itself.

When we're out of sync, the upper body disconnects from the lower body, the lower body disconnects from the ground, and the club has no relation or connection to anything fundamental, like the balance point on the feet, the physical centre of gravity or the natural centre line of the body.

Movements remain arbitrary without anything more solid or dependable than an ever-changing mind and fluctuating emotions.

Relating the mind to the physical body (rather than simply thinking about technique) is a very subtle distinction but one that actually assists the delivery of natural, connected and coordinated movement. All the trouble in golf arises from trying to make it happen by thinking about the movement, analysing various swing positions and tweaking grip, stance and swing thoughts in those very moments over the ball when you could be working to invite the inner set-up to appear. We'll look at this more closely in Chapter Ten.

Your body knows all about the kinetic chain, escalation, torque, rotation and ground force energy; it understands these things using a language that the mind simply cannot penetrate and will seamlessly act according to these laws every time your mind and body are related.

Conversely, the more you try to recreate the perfect shot without acknowledging the truth of how it manifested in the first place (i.e. from the synced-up state of *relaxed readiness*), your attempts will only take you further and further away from your natural abilities.

CHAPTER THREE

DIMINISHING RETURNS

"We do not accept that there is no relation between the thought and the body. The thought turns around and goes its own way. The body does not care and waits for something to be asked of it. For a relation to appear, there needs to be a movement of one toward the other."

Jeanne de Salzmann

Early on in my exploration of how certain principles from martial arts like Tai Chi could benefit golfers, I was struck again and again when looking through golf magazines that the writers of these articles seemed to be omitting some fundamental things which I felt, in light of my background, needed to be put in place before movement of any kind can be learned or executed, especially under pressure.

While they had some interesting and useful things to say about the technical aspects of swinging the club and the different swing positions a professional player might achieve and which the amateur should seek to replicate, it nevertheless seemed as if they were trying to put together a jigsaw puzzle without having all the pieces.

A further two decades of research, development and working with golfers of all ages and abilities haven't changed this opinion; if anything, they have strengthened it.

It's my belief that conventional golf coaching (and sports coaching *per se*) starts from the wrong premise, a premise or assumption that compounds the inherent disconnection of the mind and body, as it trains the mental game and technique separately. I'm not apportioning blame except perhaps to say that the way the modern game of golf is taught, discussed and analysed has become so left-brain that it's in danger of missing the point about what constitutes a connected swing. Concentrating on the minutiae of technique has stopped coaches, players and commentators seeing the big picture.

Older coaches seem to have more instinct and intuition about the swing than those in the modern game who rely on computer analysis and motion sensor cameras to capture what previous generations have gleaned simply by looking and listening.

Connected Golf seeks to bring a new model and new language for helping golfers understand what constitutes the effortless shot and which techniques can be employed by coaches and players alongside both the modern and classic approaches to the game. In some cases, it can even replace these.

For most players, however, swing coaching remains essential to their development, just as working out in the gym is necessary to get lean and strong. Yet without doing this *bodymind* work for inner connection alongside practising your technique, trouble abounds when you try taking your game to the course.

You've only got to look at today's elite to see the truth of this; in one tournament, a player might win, and in the next, they miss the cut, so what hope is there for the amateur? There is far less consistency now than there was before the explosion of the technical instruction industry, and drowning in all this information nullifies any hope of inner alignment or relaxed readiness in the moments before the shot is taken.

What we've learned so far about the mind-body connection is that (i) we rarely have it, (ii) even when we do, it's extremely tenuous and lasts for a matter of moments, and (iii) by using certain principles and practices we can encourage it to appear, thus allowing connected movement to ensue.

Looking at the art, science and sport of golf from my vantage point in the soft-style Chinese martial arts, it struck me so often when flicking through golf magazines at the beginning of my exploration that golfers are asked to do the impossible from their very first lesson, i.e. wield a 45" titanium shaft driver to strike at a ball 1.68" in diameter, hitting it towards a distant target.

Moreover, golfers are expected to do this without any basic training on balance, breathing or body-alignment, no knowledge of the pivot-point of rotation, and nothing at all on the mind-body connection and the inner state that all martial artists know is a prerequisite in preparation for connected movement.

To illustrate, let me tell you a little about the first Tai Chi class I attended in the East End of London way back in 1987. After guiding us through some warming-up exercises, the instructor took up a motionless stance with his feet shoulder-width apart, his knees slightly bent, his chest and his shoulders relaxed while his arms were held at chest height as if holding a large ball. The back of his head was lifted as if he was suspended from above by an invisible thread. He looked strong yet relaxed, and his expression was one of leisurely concentration.

All the members of the class took up the same posture, and there we were for at least the next 20 minutes. It was quite an experience!

I came to understand the stance by various names such as I Chuan (Yiquan) or Zhan Zhuang (literally 'standing like a post') which is just one of hundreds of different stance-keeping postures that form the basis of the many martial arts systems of the world.

Figure 1: Tai Chi 'Single Whip' posture

In traditional martial arts training, for instance, if you went to the Wudang or Shaolin temples today, you'd be expected to practise daily stance-keeping for at least 18 months before doing any 'empty-hand' drills like forms or katas, following which you'd then work on your empty-hand drills for another 18 months before picking up a weapon like a staff, broadsword or double-edged sword.

The swords themselves would initially be light and made of wood before progressing to heavier metal weapons. The training is approached in this order for many reasons, all of which can be useful for your golf performance.

First, the practitioner has to learn how to be connected in stillness: that's connecting the mind to the body, the attention to the breathing, the balance point to the floor, the upper body to the lower body, the centre line to the body's horizontal sphere.

Next, the practitioner learns how to retain these connections, the posture, breathing, balance point, centre line and so forth *while they are moving*, doing simple things at first like slow walking, and slow punching while listening to their own body and allowing the pressure of the ground to act on the centre of gravity, which, in turn, causes the upper body to rotate. All of this is done while maintaining a level of inner stillness so the mind can be related to the body, enhancing the delivery of fluid motion.

Finally, approximately three years after the start of training, the practitioner can pick up a weapon and wield it with an impressive level of internalised skill as the *bodymind* has been trained to such a degree that they are now capable of moving a short staff or a broadsword with the same whole-body unity and power which they use to move their arms and legs in form work and sparring (throwing kicks and punches).

Unfortunately in golf, after three years of learning nothing but swing positions and possibly picking up a few mental game tips, nine out of ten golfers plateau; the lucky ones level out but don't really progress, while the unlucky ones, by devouring more and more information about technique, actually get worse.

Rather than simply stopping this tendency to deteriorate, the aim of this book is to help your game evolve by showing that golf is really a set of movements similar to those in other sports and everyday life (and of course, the martial arts) and that these fundamental movements can not only be trained but called into action by developing an internal alignment which then allows the body to respond to intention.

Thinking about your technique is not a real and direct experience of the body or of movement but is an *idea about movement that will take place in a few moments*.

Trying to get it right by thinking and analysing and then getting frustrated when the shot doesn't go the way you wanted it to all but cancels out the potential wisdom of the joined-up *bodymind*.

The case for practising stance-keeping to bring the mind and body into some kind of unity and improve your golf performance isn't hard to make. Many of my students, including tour professionals, have benefited greatly from just 20 minutes practice a day, which has helped them feel 'calm and powerful' over the ball in tournament pressure and release their swing without the usual nagging doubts. There are full details on all the training given throughout this book in Part Three.

Alongside any instruction you receive from a swing professional, the lessons from **Connected Golf** will help give your body some direct feeling instructions to which technical skills can be anchored; these will become like the parameters within which your swing can be locked.

Without this conjoining of technical instruction with some fundamental principles of movement, the law of diminishing returns will undoubtedly hijack your game. This law states that at some point, any investment of time, money and effort leads to a downwards spiral of fewer and fewer returns so that, eventually, the effort put in outweighs the rewards.

To demonstrate, let's have a look at two common scenarios that affect all players from competitive amateurs to the world elite and which can be solved by adopting this new paradigm.

SCENARIO 1 – "WHY ISN'T MY RANGE SWING TRANSFERRABLE TO THE COURSE?"

Let's start with the most common frustration, and that is, taking your range swing into the game. In practice sessions, with a coach, away from the spectators and the pressure of competition, your golf swing is fluid, sometimes even languid, with a lovely tempo and a pure, clean strike of the ball. You feel nicely balanced, there is a good release and follow-through and the various swing positions form a seamlessly connected whole.

Yet under pressure, whether that's the Masters, your first pro-am event or simply fellow club members watching from the clubhouse, your swing no longer reflects your true abilities. Moreover, once you begin analysing and reworking your technique in the hope of getting your groove back, it seems to disintegrate even further.

SCENARIO 2 – "WHY IS MY PRACTICE SWING DIFFERENT TO MY ACTUAL SHOT-MAKING?"

This second most common complaint from amateur and professional golfers alike goes something like this. You stand behind the ball and take one or two practice swings as part of your pre-shot routine or preparation. You have a full backswing, a good rhythm and impact position and you follow through well.

Moments later, you address the ball, ready to take your shot, but this time you shorten your backswing, force the start of the downswing with your shoulder, raise your head, feel unbalanced and hit a really bad drive.

What is it that changes in these scenarios, and how can you bridge the all-important gap between swinging easy when there's nothing at stake and making a real hash of it when it matters most?

In *Connected Golf*, we're going to look at this phenomenon very closely and find the solution. I've watched countless students make a lovely flowing practice swing only for their technique to fail miserably when a few moments later they step up to the ball and take the shot for real. Yes, the presence of the little white ball seems to change things, but what, exactly?

Everybody in the golf industry will go over the swing, the various positions, the grip, the plane, the impact position etc., but what I've tried to encourage my students to do is look a bit deeper at what's changing, not externally in movement, but internally.

Just as a boxing fight is won or lost in the moment the two pugilists set eyes on each other, your golf shot will either connect or fragment depending on your inner state in the stillness before movement begins.

Mainstream and even left of centre coaches will talk about 'fixing' common swing faults, and as we've already touched upon, media analysis and golf journalists invariably talk about a player's technique breaking down. Yet, as ever when shifting paradigms, it's definitely worth reviewing this.

It's highly doubtful that in the time between your warm-up on the range and standing on the first tee, or especially in the brief moments between taking your practice swings and the actual shot, you've somehow forgotten how to swing a golf club. No, what's changed is your internal state, which aggravates the nervous system, activates the worry brain and nullifies the mind-body connection.

Please note this is *not* a psychological state that changes, but a biochemical reaction to pressure, i.e. the 'stress-response', which I have explored extensively in my book **Breathe Golf**.

TRY THIS NO. 3
A NEW LOOK AT YOUR PRACTICE SWINGS

Take two practice swings, then step up to the ball and take your shot; notice what subtle changes take place in your mind, body and breathing when you're over the ball, whether it's a feeling of tightness, nervous tension, a loss of balance or overthinking, any and all of which will affect how your body moves.

The training in this book is to help you keep the same inner state or conditions no matter the situation, maintaining alignment between your inner world and the desired manifestation of movement.

You can also do this exercise with a golf buddy, noticing (without criticising) the changes that take place in each other's breathing, balance, tightness of grip, stiffness in the upper body and so on, before taking the shot as opposed to the practice swings.

When working together, you can try slowing down your set-up and swing while you both keep an eye on any inner disruptions caused by the presence of the golf ball.

To follow on from this exercise, let's make another couple of distinctions between the old world and this new paradigm. First, let's look at the difference between the way your mind is used for practice and how it works best during play. In the mainstream approach, there is little to distinguish between these, and it's assumed that the part of your mind used to hone technical points on the range is the same part of the mind that can execute this in a real-time competitive situation. But it isn't.

In terms of helping or hindering golf performance, we can take a very simple look at the various parts of the brain, including the worry brain or analytical mind (pre-frontal cortex), the motor system and the calming brain or occipital lobe, which activates the alpha-waves that appear in deep meditation and during the experience of flow.

We can group this brief study under the umbrella term of biochemistry (brain-body chemistry), which controls the functioning of your nervous system from the 'fight-flight-freeze' of the stress-response to the relaxation response.

When you're practising golf, tinkering with your grip, adjusting the mechanics of your swing or understanding more about the physics of the game, including the arc or plane of the club and ball flight laws, your analytical mind can be extremely useful. It's also necessary for course management, strategy and positive thinking.

However, over-using this aspect of thinking, i.e. analysis, when you're on the golf course, activates the worry brain and induces the stress-response, which signals the further fragmentation of the *bodymind*, and the breakdown of connected movement.

As one of my students pointed out, his experience of the game before he began to train his mind-body connection was that he 'hardly ever played golf when on the course' because his experience was always one of anxiety, self-doubt and frustration.

During play and under pressure, you need to use the part of the brain that can help release natural movement by learning to switch off or at least quieten down the other areas of the mind which want to take over and try to control your movement.

When you reduce thinking and don't try so hard, the worry brain stops dominating, and the calming brain comes to the fore. This enables a more joined-up experience of a quieter mind and the motor brain working in unison.

When the thinking brain is quiet or indeed when it goes offline for a few moments, as happens very often during meditation, a more Zen-like or unified brain appears where thoughts seem to move to the back of the head, and the volume of the inner dialogue is significantly reduced. Standing over the ball with these inner conditions in place enables the part of the brain responsible for movement to take its instructions directly without any self-interference.

We'll look at various ways you can help this process (remembering that you can't force it), including shifting your attention from swing thoughts to swing feelings.

Swing thoughts are a huge issue that's crept into the modern game, and I often wonder who came up with this concept and also what would happen should they find themselves alone one night in the club car park with a group of angry golfers.

As we're beginning to see, swing thoughts can so easily degenerate into analysis of individual swing positions, and it's hard to understand why the emphasis shifted, especially as swing feelings are something the great Jack Nicklaus used and wrote about during his unsurpassed career. If it was good enough for the Golden Bear, why was it abandoned in favour of 'thinking about movement'?

Swing thoughts per se have no useful connection to the body; they are simply a list of instructions for the mind, just like a checklist. Worse still, they are ideas about movement that the golfer is hoping to perform in the next few moments, without anything but the changing mind and fluctuating attention to hold them together.

Without interventions such as the Standing Practice trained by martial artists and the connections that are developed as a result, i.e. balance and rotating from the centre of gravity, and as we'll see later, things like joint-stacking, fascia-stretching, and, holding the centre line, the golf swing remains something arbitrary, almost ethereal, which can't be grasped and held onto.

This, of course, leads us back to the default state of thinking too much and trying to control movement, which hinders any ability you might have to let your body move naturally and freely, just like it did on the range or during your practice swings.

When thoughts take over, it's not only the connection to the body that's at stake but also the athlete's relationship to intention.

As I wrote in my eBook *The Practice of High-Performance*, "Intention has nothing to do with the mind, at least not the analytical part of the mind and as such it cannot be summoned by going through a checklist of points about body positions or the movement you wish to perform... Intention primes the body for movement and results in a chain of events which could be summed up in three words – intention, activation, movement – and so long as this sequence or natural circuit is not interrupted or broken by analytical thinking, your movement will flow."

The sad thing for so many players who love the game is that they don't see or experience the golf swing as a natural movement like kicking a ball or hitting a moving ball with a bat or racket. I hope to demonstrate why golf can and should be a reaction to intent, as it is for many other sports, and that further, you can use your fundamental movement skills from other sports you play to improve.

Connected Golf aims to offer competitive players of the game a series of simple threads that can run through everything from the range to the course and into the tournament.

The foundations of this alternative approach are timeless. As we'll see in the next chapter, while technical trends come and go, certain principles of movement are fundamental and remain true whatever the sport, whatever the situation and always begin in the moments *before* the athlete starts moving. They are what you should work with, focus on, train, pay attention to, both as internal and external structures within which your own natural swing can be anchored.

Let me reiterate that swing coaching and mental game coaching definitely have their place in the development of a player; they are as important as strength and conditioning, nutrition and supplementation, stretching and hydration, but I've seen so many golfers disenchanted, fed-up and frustrated that their games aren't getting any better and in a lot of cases are getting worse, and I've spent a couple of decades working out exactly why this is so.

I also have several close associations with PGA and WGTF coaches whom I like and respect very much but who are training with me for the very reason we see time and time again in the modern game: knowledge of technique does not equal player ability.

This book asks you to forego the emphasis on mental and technical coaching alone and awaken the dormant *bodymind* by giving you ways to train based on centuries-old principles of mind, breathing and movement.

You can't make the perfect shot happen; all you can do is prepare the ground for it to arise, but if you can work towards this, you are virtually guaranteed to play a better, more rewarding and enjoyable game.

CHAPTER FOUR

A CHANGE OF PERSPECTIVE

*"Technique is a trap; style is a prison.
Kung-fu is meant to liberate."*

Wong Jack Man

In **Connected Golf,** we're re-looking at the mainstream assumptions upon which coaches are expected to teach and players are expected to perform; many of these will be turned upside down in our continuing exploration to discover the truth of the effortless golf shot, a foundation upon which the whole game turns.

As we're learning, a different perspective is useful and perhaps needed, now more than ever, and I hope what's offered here can be considered categorical, based as it is on over three decades of training and teaching centuries-old disciplines of the mind-body connection.

From this vantage point, we've seen the following:

Controlling biochemistry takes precedence over psychology and positive thinking. It doesn't necessarily replace it, − all things have their designated role − but it certainly takes precedence during play. The brain-body chemistry triggers the stress-response and all ensuing forms of self-interference like overthinking and trying too hard, which manifest in a poor shot. The result of this biochemical response is the breakdown of fluid movement, but the origins are in the nervous system and not in the realm of the mind; the mind simply follows and creates coherence with the feelings of anxiety. This is a very important distinction.

There are certain fundamental principles which are related to movement and take precedence over technique. Again, they don't replace it, but they are imperative and override trends and fads that come and go. We'll be exploring these throughout the book but simply put, they can be divided into two pillars.

The first pillar is awareness of breathing, which helps to lessen feelings of anxiety and reduce unnecessary thinking. This was explored in my previous book **Breathe Golf**.

The second pillar is the foundations of natural movement, which we're now examining and applying specifically to golf. These have been discovered, refined and honed by successive generations of martial arts families and schools, for instance, those of various Tai Chi lineages, all working according to the same principles. These will form our benchmark for further exploration in Part Two.

Compare this with the lack of consensus among golf teaching professionals as to the core components of the swing, for instance, how the take-away begins and where the transition is initiated from, whether it's a one plane or two plane movement, let alone what constitutes what might be termed the classic or modern versions. Add to this the fact that there are so many different examples of the golf swing on the elite tour today, and it becomes hard to see any underlying principles at all.

I can't help but think about the parable of the blind men and the elephant! This ancient story attributed to Buddhist and Hindu texts tells us about a group of blind men who heard that a strange animal, called an elephant, had been brought to the town, although none of them knew anything about it. Out of curiosity, they decided to inspect it using the sense of touch as looking at the elephant to determine its shape and form was denied to them. So, they sought it out, and when they found it, they started moving their hands around the elephant's large mass. The first, whose hand landed on the trunk, said, "This animal resembles a huge snake," and the second, whose hand reached its ear, said it seemed the elephant was like a fan that could be used to ward off flies and keep cool. As for the third person, whose hand was upon its leg, it seemed the elephant was a pillar similar to a tree trunk. The blind man who placed his hand upon its side said the elephant "is a wall" and yet another who felt its tail described it as a rope. The last felt its tusk, stating the elephant was smooth and shaped like a spear. As none of the blind men could agree on exactly what the elephant was, the exploration turned into a fierce argument, with none of them trusting what the other ones said.

What this story illustrates is that subjective realisations are only true in part and that a bigger, more objective reality is often hidden from our limited perceptions.

In golf, there are so many contradictory theories and opinions, but we'll see that certain laws regarding complex movement remain timeless and further that they apply to all sports.

When we apply them to golf, you learn to train the mind and body in specific ways, so they can join together to release a more natural, consistent and repeatable swing.

Understanding this offers a bigger picture that can help to dispel much of the current disagreement in the industry and give some definite parameters within which individual teaching styles and methods can flourish.

A common factor among many of the top swing coaches is the way they actively promote the idea that they have sole possession of the secret to better golf, a secret which they're prepared to pass on to high-paying clients. These coaches rarely share their methods with their fellow coaches and, in fact, rubbish the ideas posited by others in the same profession.

This creates ongoing disagreement about what constitutes the ideal swing and is as confusing to the elite player as it is to the committed amateur.

While there are lots of great and innovative theories, when you look at the key causes of effortless movement, many coaches with a specific insight into the swing or impact position expand their particular idea to such a point of detail and analysis that it consequently can do more harm than good.

The swing is always deconstructed and interpreted from the point of view of what was wrong with it, without acknowledging that the many and varied faults which show up in motion are already in place at the set-up. A coach may understand something about the similarities of certain movements, for instance, how a golf swing is similar to driving a nail with a hammer, but only when we engage the balance point, as identified in the martial arts, can the body respond naturally and powerfully to the intention to strike at rather than swing at the ball.

When interpretations deviate from the accepted principles honed in the Eastern arts, the understanding of the key drivers that constitute the perfect swing get lost in translation. As with the parable of the blind men and the elephant, many of the world's top swing coaches have a piece of the puzzle but not the whole picture.

Nowhere is this more clearly demonstrated than in the desperate plight of the elite player who has lost form and changes their swing coach in an attempt to get back in the game.

When a player isn't performing well, they will find another coach who offers a variation on movement positions or the swing shape in the hope of finding the cure, the key to fixing the fault or faults in their swing. Yet this is often nothing better than a different set of compensations, and while the new secret gleaned from the new coach might work on the practice range, the player may have limited success with it in their next tournament.

There's a reason for this.

As we're becoming all too aware, the secret to better golf does not lie in learning ever more about technique or even in changing one's technique, but in the two-fold path of bringing the mind into closer harmony with the body and training the body in some very simple, yet fundamental skills, which will enhance the delivery of natural and instinctive movement, especially when it needs to withstand the onslaught of pressure.

The golf swing of the player who wants to find their groove again having lost it, would then be easier to fine-tune and replicate once certain fundamentals are firmly understood and in place.

A couple of examples of how these fundamentals of movement can support the modern approach to the game, and which we'll explore in greater detail in Part Two, are in regard to the concepts around spiral motion and compression (of the body, not the golf ball!).

One of the world's top coaches promotes the idea of the golf swing being like a spiral staircase to encourage a three-dimensional as opposed to lateral movement. It's a brilliant and useful insight, and yet the incorporation of simple principles from Tai Chi or Aikido, which are both famous for developing rotational or spiral force and give specific guidelines on how to do this in the most effective way, wouldn't go amiss!

For instance, without an understanding of the differing qualities upper and lower body must have in order to allow a smooth escalation from ground to wrists, the instruction and swing thoughts used to deliberately create the kinetic chain actually go against principles of natural movement.

Another top coach has brought the useful notion of the physical compression of the upper body into the transition as a vital component of transferring what he calls 'swing energy' into the ball.

Again, this is a fantastic insight, but even a cursory nod to the internal arts can help the player train their body correctly, specifically by understanding how structural power moves upwards while simultaneously the power of gravity moves downwards and, moreover, how these opposing forces are resolved by using the t'an tien, which combines these forces together with rotational movement, as in a devastating kung-fu punch!

As an interesting aside, let's find out how one of the world's greatest kung-fu fighters, Bruce Lee, described this phenomenon.

He explained that being hit with a Karate punch (a hard, external fighting art) is like being hit with an iron bar, but being hit with a kung-fu punch was like being hit with an iron ball on the end of a chain. The latter is going to penetrate more deeply into the body and be far more devastating to the opponent. This is exactly the motion you're looking for in the golf swing, a sort of whip-like, elastic energy that accelerates through impact.

Seen in this way, it's not so much swing energy as ground force energy that's transferred in a natural escalation from the feet and through the waist before passing through the wrists (which will unhinge naturally if the other components are adhered to!) and finally through the ball.

Yet ground force cannot be obtained with a tight upper body, raised shoulders or shallow breathing and certainly not without adhering to the structural points that lie within the body's fascia, from the sternum to the psoas and the arch of the foot.

All of the principles from the centuries-old *soft-style* or internal martial arts are verified by modern biomechanics and sports science, particularly when we look at the connective tissue, which not only runs up the front and down the back of the body but also spirals around the mid and centre lines in two different directions.

Connected Golf shows you how the body has been trained for hundreds of years to harness these forces and how to bring this into your golf practice and game.

The choice is clear. You can either train your body to allow such forces as rotation and compression to occur as a result of certain inner alignments and conditions, or you can force them, which means that under pressure, you're in danger of moving further and further away from anything resembling natural and connected movement.

For instance, so many of my students, even though they might have been sceptical at first, have noticed significant improvements in their performance after simply doing 10 minutes Standing Meditation every day for just a few weeks.

Here's what Scott P. from Pittsburgh, who we heard from earlier, has to say about this:

> *"I have been working with Jayne for the last few months. I am both an avid golfer and trap shooter with a primary goal of gaining greater satisfaction in both of these sports.*
>
> *"We started first with the fundamental base of learning, both seated and Standing Meditation. I have been doing both on a daily basis. Initially, I found it hard to fathom how both forms of meditation would benefit my game.*
>
> *"Just recently, I have begun to see the results of my practice. When taking a golf or trap shot, I feel a sense of relaxed readiness with my upper body centred over my lower body. This has allowed me to stay in my posture from the start to finish of my shot. I have noticed a greater feel for the shot, and I get the sense that I am observing myself make an effortless move. I am definitely less focused on the outcome and more on the process and feeling for the shot."*

Another dramatic change in our perspective has been to look at the role stillness plays in releasing complex motions like the golf swing. Golfers and other athletes rarely analyse the quality of their shot-making based on the quality of their breathing or their inner quiet in the moments before movement commences, yet it's vital that we examine this in order to discover the truth about movement per se and movement under pressure in particular.

Figure 2: Optical Illusion – two heads or a vase?

To this end, here's an analogy that might help; it gives precedence to what we might call 'the *operator* of the golfing machine' rather than the machine itself. What do I mean by this?

Instead of our focus of attention being on the golfer's mental state and the various positions we're told constitute a golf swing, we're going to shift our perspective so that we concentrate on the flip side of this coin, just as if we changed our perspective from seeing the silhouette of a vase to seeing the *two profiles* in this classic optical illusion.

In **Breathe Golf,** we touched briefly on Murphy's law which states that when applied to anything of a mechanical nature, "if something can go wrong, it will go wrong." From the feedback I've received from golfers around the world, it seems this struck a familiar chord, to wit: the never-ending tweaking of your golf technique, only to find that as soon as one part gets fixed, something else breaks down. It's a useful way of reiterating the inherent disconnect and how this leads to diminishing returns.

In this book, we're going to use another comparison to gain a new perspective on golf, which is waiting to welcome you into a better and more enjoyable game, and that's the difference between 'the golfing machine' and the operator of the machine, i.e. the golfer.

I'm not dissing Homer Kelley's book of the same name, just the assumption that getting various swing positions 'right', is the be all and end all of good technique. Instead, I want to bring you, the golfer, as the actual operator of the golfing machine, into the equation, but as you're discovering, instead of looking purely at your mental state, we're going to look a bit deeper at what we might call your inner state or mind-body connection.

Essentially, the more connected the operator (golfer), the more connected the workings of the machine (swing positions). The machine, in this instance, is quite literally in the operator's hands, and when the operator is out-of-sorts, pent up, frustrated, worried or anxious, the machine won't be able to function properly.

With a quietly composed operator, one who's paying attention to their body, their breathing, the pressure of their grip, the feeling of their feet on the ground, without worrying about how the machine's going to perform in the next few moments, it allows the movements of the machine to be more fluid, more seamless, more connected.

Just yesterday, I was speaking with one of my long-term students on a video call, and he said what so many have reported, and that is, when he tries too hard to get it right, he feels shut away in a box, worried and anxious, and his body feels tight. When he can let go of this and stay with the simple yet fundamental awareness of himself standing over the ball in a state of relaxed readiness, it allows his body to do what it knows how to do, unfettered by the control freak mind.

Technical thoughts, however brilliant, are just ideas about movement; they are not the actual experience, feeling or sensation either of movement or of the physical body and thus, they give the machine nothing concrete to work with, just a changing menu of instructions coupled with varying mood swings.

If, instead, the operator can bring their attention and awareness to their own body, including feeling properly balanced and being physically centred, and if they can stay with this and become more connected internally, the golf swing stands a better chance of being a unified movement instead of a series of poorly executed fragmented parts.

What we see externally in the manifestation of movement is always the result of what's taking place inside the golfer before they start their swing. Technical understanding and mental fortitude are useful and necessary, but it's not where your efforts to become a great golfer should end. In fact, on their own or even coupled with interventions from the so-called mental game, they're a dead end, as these stories illustrate.

Fred and Mitchell (not their real names) are both professional golf coaches who've been suffering with chronic anxiety and the yips, respectively.

Fred is a really exceptional young guy in the Netherlands who has often come so close to a perfect understanding of how, when his mind quietens down, his golf swing is more connected, but he's unable to let go of all the technical knowledge in his head so most of the time all he feels standing over the ball is fear. In fact, the word he's used to describe his state is 'terrified'. He no longer knows what to do, cannot trust his own swing, doesn't know which theory to follow, how to take the club away, how to relate to the club or bring the club to impact the ball and has had one disastrous round after another when playing competitively.

Mitchell's game has also gone south, and for him, the anxiety caused by trying to get it right and, moreover, the pressure of being seen as someone who should be able to play well (after all, he knows everything there is to know about the golf swing) has meant that he's suffered from the yips and for over 15 years has been unable to play in tournaments against others, even though he runs a successful coaching business in Germany.

Their stories are not uncommon. At times I've even facilitated groups of coaches, and while everybody in the conference room might know the minutiae of swing mechanics, not a single person is able to take this onto the course, especially under pressure. So, what's missing here? Something's seriously adrift, and unfortunately, it filters down to the grassroots level of the game, as the following example demonstrates.

Tim was in his mid-teens and a really promising junior elite player who had a natural, easy swing in practice but whose game had a tendency to fall apart in tournaments.

Tim's father brought him to see me, having done the rounds with all the local swing coaches and psychologists, as it seemed that nobody in the industry could help him. While his swing was near perfect on the range, it was a mess under pressure, and the worse he played, the more frustrated he felt until he was on the verge of giving up the game completely.

When I met Tim at the club and saw him swing on the practice area, I couldn't help but notice two crucial things. First, he wasn't balanced properly, and secondly, he was holding his breath for the entire duration of the movement.

Let's look at these in turn.

I've lost count of the number of students, even those from other professional sports coming into the game, as well as golfers who've played over several decades, who've told me they've never felt balanced over the ball. Yet, according to natural movement principles (which we'll look at closely in Chapter Eight), there is a point on the feet where it's most favourable to place your weight for the greatest stability and connection to the ground.

If Hogan, Nicklaus and many other legends of golf have told us that the swing starts from the feet upwards, echoing what generations of martial arts practitioners have advocated about movement, then if a player isn't balanced at set-up, their swing will at best be nothing more than a controlled mistake.

Add pressure to this equation, and it starts to come apart.

Couple this with Tim holding his breath; this placed his energy and centre of gravity in his chest, further disconnecting him from the ground and initiating the stress-response in his nervous system. Compounded over a round, this led to feelings of anxiety, thoughts spiralling out of control, an increasingly rushed shot preparation and a complete deterioration in performance.

Externally it looked like Tim's technique had come apart, he had some technical issue which needed fixing or he had too many or the wrong kind of swing thoughts or not enough self-belief, but in truth it was because the foundations or two pillars of movement were not in place in the moments before his swing began.

It's unfortunate that not only could these issues not be resolved using the conventional approach, but they weren't even noticed or acknowledged, and so the poor boy's head was simply filled with more technical instructions and tips about positive thinking.

TRY THIS NO. 4
REVIEWING YOUR LAST COMPETITION

Review your last competition as impartially as possible from the point of view of all you've learned so far about this different perspective on golf. Sum up your good shots and bad shots by reflecting on your inner state before taking the shot. How connected were your mind and body? Were you aware of your body or just technical thoughts? Were you breathing or holding your breath? Were you comfortable over the ball, or did you rush? How quiet was your mind when standing over the ball? What happened to your inner state as the pressure mounted?

It's hard to let go of convention, but many golfers, even experienced and well-respected coaches and those on the professional playing circuit, have bravely taken this path before you. In an attempt to move forward with their game, they have gone back in time to centuries-old wisdom about how to connect the mind, breathing and movement.

Slowly, over weeks and months of committed practice to the drills and exercises we're covering in this book, every golfer who's taken the time to develop these Performance Practices has experienced a significant reduction in the tension allied to performing under pressure.

Those who've been teaching feel ready to get back to playing in tournaments; those who play in competitions have started to feel calm and confident, knowing how to anchor their attention and their movement in the here and now, instead of being overloaded with information. They have started to feel 'in the game' rather than complaining that their body feels tight or their golf swing feels weird, or they are suffering with anxiety.

Even golfers who've played and taught over six decades have seen how the simplest awareness, when developed through consistent training, shows extraordinarily subtle correspondences between the pace of breathing, their inner rhythm and the tempo of their swing.

By feeling the difference in their movement when they let go of trying too hard and stay within certain physical parameters, they're beginning to recognise when flow appears, and one after another has told me that the feelings they're now training and honing are the very same feelings experienced when they've played their best golf.

Golf is not a new set of movements but uses principles that are common across all sports; as such, golfers don't need to create a new set of thoughts to steer the movement. The kinetic chain is a natural sequence of events in the body that will occur effortlessly as a result of establishing the two pillars that are fundamental to all movement, all of the time.

The synced-up *bodymind* that results from establishing these pillars before movement commences is something that many of us have experienced in the heightened state of flow or the zone. Although it's usually touched upon by accident, we can increase our access rate to this state through a certain type of training.

Understanding this phenomenon has been a three-decades-long search, and I believe the athlete's role in this new paradigm is not only to be super fit and learn the technical aspects of their craft but to then set about creating the right internal conditions that allow technique to be released naturally and spontaneously, under the pressure of competition.

It's not the athlete's job to try and make the perfect shot or movement routine happen but to practise creating the right inner conditions that allow effortless movement to emerge, and it needs practising and training to override aeons of the 'fight-flight-freeze' response and the incessant inner dialogue.

It also needs consistent training to help overcome the default tendency to start searching for a swing when technique *seems* to fall apart, but this can be halted and reversed when the right inner conditions have once again been established.

From my research, I've identified three different levels of golf, which take into account the inherent disconnect, the diminishing returns offered by the mainstream and what's possible when we change our perspective!

Let's take a look at these now.

PERFORMANCE PYRAMID

CONNECTED GOLF

GOOD DAYS, BAD DAYS

SEARCH FOR A SWING

Figure 3: Performance Pyramid – the three levels of golf

CHAPTER FIVE

THREE LEVELS OF PERFORMANCE

"Only connect."

E.M. Forster

Since you are reading this book, it's safe to assume you're either interested in becoming a better golfer or you're frustrated at your current level of performance and think you should be doing better. Perhaps your game has plateaued after years of taking lessons, buying all the latest equipment, building a practice area in your back garden and watching all those instructional videos online. It might also be that you're not only failing to see any improvement but are actually sliding backwards. Sure, there are days when it all comes together, and your scores are reasonable, but you also have days when nothing works, and you just can't figure out what's going on.

It's more than likely you've hit some incredible shots that reaffirm your love for the game, and yet as soon as you feel that you're finally on the threshold of playing to your potential, things start to unravel.

If this sounds like your experience, you may have run up against the Performance Paradoxes, which were first mentioned in my book *Breathe Golf*.

These paradoxes are as follows.

Performance Paradox No. 1 – 'The harder you try, the worse it gets'.

Performance Paradox No. 2 – 'Training a pattern is counter to effortless motion'.

Performance Paradox No. 3 – 'To obtain the desired result, focus on the process'.

As frustrating as they can be, these paradoxes are quite natural; they exist in and of themselves in any situation where the performance of complex movement is at stake, particularly under pressure. We'll be looking at each of them in turn throughout this chapter.

You may also have come face to face with the fluctuating state of your mind, body and emotions, which demonstrates the basic lack of consistency characteristic of all human beings.

We are more cerebral one day, more emotional the next; some days we have energy, then we feel lethargic, we have attention and focus, and then we start daydreaming. It could be down to our biorhythms, things going on in our personal life, work stress, lack of sleep, health issues and so forth, but they also show how everything within us is in perpetual motion. As such, attempting to pin down a complex sequence of movement such as the golf swing into a watertight formula that we can repeat with exactitude time and time again is really a fool's game.

This realisation can be extraordinary and liberating; indeed, it is one of the fascinations with golf and shows why it lends itself so well to the Eastern way of viewing the world.

No two games are the same, and no two shots are the same. Even if you played the same course at the same time every day, just like an artist who paints the same scene over and over in all seasons and all weather, what you'd witness would be a constantly changing kaleidoscope.

Within all these variations though, some things remain constant. In golf, there are ball flight laws, for instance, and in the delivery of complex movement, it's the two pillars of breathing and natural movement, and it's upon these that you need to focus your practice time and energy.

Interestingly, they are exactly the same principles you can take into your game and, even more remarkably, you can also use them to your advantage in competition.

Let's take a look into what I've identified as three distinct levels of golf, which are almost like three different games. They will help to convey the new language and paradigm **Connected Golf** is offering, so you can deflect the tendency to revert to the mainstream approach when you're in the middle of a round, rather than trusting what you've learned so far and from your own reflections on your game.

Let's begin with another game you may remember from your childhood.

'Snakes and Ladders', known originally as Moksha Patam, is an ancient Indian board game for two or more players, widely regarded today as a worldwide classic. It is played on a game board with numbered, gridded squares. A number of 'ladders' and 'snakes' are pictured on the board, each connecting two specific board squares. The object of the game is to navigate one's game piece, determined by rolls of the die, from the start (bottom square) to the finish (top square). The player is assisted by landing on a square which enables them to climb one of the ladders and hindered by landing on a square which penalises them by falling down one of the snakes.

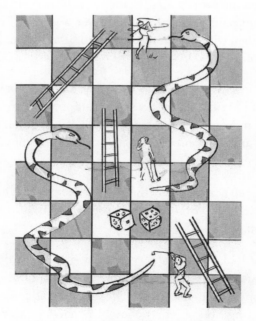

Figure 4: Golf Snakes and Ladders

It seems a similar situation abounds in the game of golf as the level of a player's performance can both accelerate (ascending the ladder) then deteriorate (descending the snake) over a season and, curiously, within the same round.

It became obvious after working with several hundred golfers of varying ages and abilities that there are indeed different levels of the game and that when players talk about golf, they're not all talking about the same thing. Instead, they fluctuate between experiencing and describing these different levels.

Here's what I've noticed.

The first or bottom level, the lowest common denominator, is a game called 'Search for a Swing'. This level is marked by a player's tendency to take the tips and tricks culture of our digital age onto the course, endlessly reworking their grip, stance and swing positions during a round. It's where the majority of 'hackers' exist alongside those who either don't want to improve or believe they can find a shortcut without putting in the necessary practice.

Unfortunately, it's also the level of the game that's played by the committed amateur and elite professional when faced with mounting pressure and, particularly, expectation. It happens when they fall out of their groove and start the damning cycle of thinking about technique and trying to tough it out mentally. Let's call this tendency the 'default state' as every player's been there.

The middle level, level two, is a markedly better game called 'Good Days, Bad Days'. This is characterised by the curious phenomenon of a player hitting some great shots only to 'snap out of it' when they notice what's going on (let's call it being in flow) and, wanting to hold onto it, they begin trying that little bit harder.

I'm sure you know what's coming next. If the player starts to get frustrated, angry or upset that they can no longer find their groove, they're in danger of falling down a snake to level one, where they start a desperate search for their swing. We've seen this so many times, even with the greatest players in the world.

The third or highest level is a game called 'Connected Golf'; it's marked by an elevated level of performance stemming from the flow-state where the player's ball-striking is sweet, and they're able to sustain this over most of the round. Even at times when a shot or two might go astray, they don't collapse, they don't search, their game doesn't deteriorate into a 'bad day'. These players understand something about how and why their swing is so connected and place their efforts on maintaining the right internal conditions that encourage this state to arise without forcing it or trying too hard.

It would be interesting to ask yourself the following questions:

Where are you on the Performance Pyramid?

Which game do you play the majority of the time?

Have you experienced all three levels at different times during your golfing life?

Do you recognise the default tendency to slide downwards when your ability to play well suddenly leaves you and you start over-trying and thinking too much?

When I've talked about the three levels with my students, they not only appreciate that it's a great summation of how their performance varies, but it also helps them to rely more on their Performance Practices on the course, especially when things start to unravel.

This is the secret of connected golf: stay connected! Or rather, when you disconnect, only seek to reconnect internally (TMB), which will take you back up the ladder, rather than looking outside yourself for the answers (CFM) and descending the snake.

The end result of the three levels is how they show up in real-time on the golf course, but the seeds of each level are planted earlier, in the way the game is taught and in how and what the player practises. Let's examine this more closely.

LEVEL ONE: SEARCH FOR A SWING

The lowest level of golf performance perfectly illustrates the first of the three Performance Paradoxes, which states that 'The harder you try, the worse it gets'. Actually, the harder you try, the worse it gets because the further away you move from the internal conditions of the mind-body connection. This level is all CFM and very little else.

As we're exploring throughout this book, the inner qualities that help give rise to TMB are characterised by a quiet mind, deep and rhythmic breathing, a sense of calm, an awareness of one's physical centre and a clarity of intent to which the body can respond, without the usual layers of self-interference which include the stress-response, too many swing thoughts and the incessant inner dialogue.

While we're back on the subject of swing thoughts, I'm often asked if these should be abandoned altogether in favour of swing feelings, and my answer is no. Swing thoughts can be useful so long as they are tied into some physical fundamentals.

If you are able to hold on mentally to helpful tips your swing professional has given you while simultaneously bringing part of your attention to your breathing and the sensation of your physical body, be it your grip or your feet on the ground, it's more than likely the thoughts you've chosen to support you can be maintained for the duration of the shot.

In level one, however, swing thoughts become a form of mental gymnastics in that they're constantly changing, both from shot to shot and, more alarmingly, during the actual swing motion itself. These players might start the backswing with a few specific thoughts in their mind, but then from the top down, these thoughts change as the attention wanders or the worry mind kicks in, or they have a better idea!

I've been contacted by so many players after their games got worse and their handicaps went up and up over the years from buying into this level. Nothing sticks following a swing lesson because it's not connected to any feeling, sensation or awareness of the physical body, just the analytical mind endlessly consuming more and more data in the hope that remembering some of it during play will help produce a flowing motion.

As we've seen, this rarely happens as the more a player knows about technique, the more trouble they have releasing their natural movement abilities. I gave you some examples of the pros and coaches I've worked with and what happens when they over-rely on the mind to recall information about movement.

Sadly, however, this isn't the end of the story for level one.

We also see this level defaulted to by some of the greatest players in the world, often when the expectation is high for them to win a particular tournament. In these situations, tee shots go astray, fairway shots are fluffed, hazards or the rough are found, three putting becomes the norm, runs of bogies are made instead of birdies, and the harder they try, and the more they think about their technique in a desperate search to find their swing, the worse it gets. Then, of course, on day two or three of the tournament, when the so-called favourite is no longer in contention, and they start to relax, their swing suddenly returns.

HOW IS THIS LEVEL COACHED?

In all likelihood, the issues affecting golfers at this level are not solely due to the industry's current approach to teaching the game (although the paradigm is surely out-of-date), but due to the information age in which we live and the average golfer's insistence on going to different coaches while simultaneously trawling the internet for instructional videos, thus overloading the mind with theory, and conflicting theories at that.

The model for this level is that of the golfing machine, to use our earlier analogy, without any attention paid to the operator of the machine. When the player tries to make changes to their swing, they will focus on individual, specific movements and try to achieve them by deliberately steering the body into position.

The player is overloaded with technical points about movement rather than concentrating on good fundamentals like the grip, set-up position and take-away.

WHAT IS THIS LEVEL'S APPROACH TO PRACTICE?

This level brings to mind all the young guys in the gym who strain into position with weights that are far too heavy, using very limited range of motion, often misunderstanding the exercise needed to target a specific muscle. They always stand out in stark contrast to the older and more seasoned weight trainers who go slowly, use perfect form and don't need to make a call, send a text or scroll through their phone between sets.

The golfer at this level spends all their spare time on the driving range. They focus on trying to get their technique right, use lots of upper body movement, swing too hard and force the ball into the air. It's doubtful that any of their shots are intentional in terms of target or distance. Their golf is often ego-driven, with very little self-awareness, and there is likely to be little interest in studying the mental game.

WHAT IS THIS LEVEL'S APPROACH TO PLAYING?

In this level, the golfer has too many ideas about how to execute the swing, and they often change their swing thoughts during a shot and tweak their swing mechanics in the middle of a round. As this level is all golfing machine, the operator (golfer) gets tied in knots mentally and is unable to release their own natural movement abilities.

This level is marked by an endless search for the right technique, never settling on any one theory, constantly fixing, fiddling and tinkering, with very little actual enjoyment of the game of golf, and little trust in one's own abilities.

WHAT HAPPENS AT THIS LEVEL UNDER PRESSURE?

I'm sure you don't need me to tell you that players at this level don't often rise to the challenge of playing under pressure; their games can completely unravel, leaving them angry, tearful, baffled and frustrated.

WHAT ARE THE ANTIDOTES TO THIS LEVEL?

Not only is this level the lowest tier of golf performance affecting the kind of player we've just heard about, but unfortunately, it's the level where good or even great players can end up once they succumb to the default tendency exacerbated by the mainstream of thinking too much and trying too hard, the classic symptoms of searching for a swing.

The antidotes to level one are to quieten the mind and calm the nervous system in an attempt to move away from CFM and towards TMB. The simple protocols in **Breathe Golf** are most suited to players trapped at this level, although a lot of effort would be required to reduce all the mental interference and learn to make everything quiet inside.

For those good and great players who end up here having fallen down a snake on our imaginary game board, the following exercise can be useful.

TRY THIS NO. 5
SMILE, BREATHE AND GO SLOWLY

This is a quote from the Vietnamese Buddhist monk Thich Nhat Hanh, which perfectly illustrates the qualities that arise from regular meditation practice. After sitting quietly for some time, practitioners often feel a sense of inner peace and joyfulness, and their movements are a lot more purposeful as the mind stays subtly connected to the actions of the body.

It can be useful to try and emulate this state. Even if you're not currently doing a regular meditation practice, you can still decide to take yourself less seriously, relax into your breathing and slow down your shot preparation and practice swings. These mindful thoughts and movements will help you move a step closer to TMB.

LEVEL TWO: GOOD DAYS, BAD DAYS

The middle level on the Performance Pyramid perfectly illustrates the second Performance Paradox, which states, 'Training a pattern is counter to effortless movement'.

Players at this level are characterised by having a good understanding of technique and an interest in game strategy and course management. They also know a good deal about sports psychology and the mental game, do plenty of gym and fitness training, possibly follow a good nutrition and supplementation plan and have a competitive spirit and a willingness to practice.

Yet level two shows how the quality of golf shots can change dramatically from moment to moment as a beautiful tee shot and par-5 birdie is followed by a run of bogies for no apparent reason.

The pure, spontaneous arising of perfection seems to be just that; it appears as if by magic in a moment of sweet connection with the ball. It's the type of shot that we heard about in Chapter One: The Effortless Shot, but then, just as mysteriously, it can disappear.

The issue becomes, what do you do next?!

For level two players, the mistaken assumptions made when the game's going well can include thoughts such as, 'It must be because I did such and such in my swing technique' or 'It's this great new 3-wood I've just bought' or 'It's because I told myself I'd hit a good shot' and so forth.

I think you know where this is going. These players (possibly you) then try to replicate the effortless shot using the current paradigm of thinking about their technique and keeping their thoughts positive.

They end up trying too hard and forcing things on the next shot, which might not come off so well, and this leads to the inevitable doubt, anxiety, frustration, even anger and the danger of defaulting to Level One: Search for a Swing.

HOW IS THIS LEVEL COACHED?

Typically, this level, which is played by the majority of competitive amateurs and elite tour professionals, entails having a swing coach and quite possibly a mental game coach or sports psychologist on their team. However, not only does this exacerbate the inherent disconnect, but it's the very old-world paradigm that I believe needs reviewing.

Coaching the mind and body separately cannot in any way lead to the regular experience of flow or the zone. Yes, it can arise in and of itself, resulting in the accidental perfect shot, but trying to recreate it by reverting to the golfing machine model of the game is like putting the cart before the horse.

Moreover, using the kind of mental game theories useful for life coaching and business development can prove as damaging to level two players as the insistence many of today's swing coaches have on using titbits of Eastern philosophy without any real understanding.

It can be harmful for players when swing coaches give off-the-cuff tips like 'keep breathing and stay present'. Without following that advice themselves, coaches who talk about such things without doing the practice simply transfer ideas they have about mindfulness into the minds of their students.

This simply adds more layers of thinking and additional swing thoughts.

WHAT IS THIS LEVEL'S APPROACH TO PRACTICE?

This level is practised by taking lessons and working the swing at the driving range; players might also psych-up before a tournament in an attempt to be mentally tough, and they may also have read something about 'breathing techniques' or picked up a few mindfulness tips.

Yet what's practised doesn't generally equate with what the golfer brings into their game; the focus is on swing mechanics and mind strategies rather than performance fundamentals, so it's easy for their games to descend into searching for a swing.

WHAT IS THIS LEVEL'S APPROACH TO PLAYING?

When it goes well for a player at level two, all's well, and there's no need to think anything other than that their approach is working; when it goes wrong, and they stick with this same approach, the tendency is to slide back down the snake to level one.

WHAT HAPPENS AT THIS LEVEL UNDER PRESSURE?

The big, glaring danger here is a basic lack of self-awareness (I'm rushing, holding my breath, I don't feel comfortable over the ball, I'm gripping the club too tightly) and a mistrust of one's natural abilities as the biochemistry takes over; anxiety is aroused, the mind seeks coherence, and all the mental interference is summoned so that the body can no longer move freely.

Any ideas about mindfulness or positive thinking tend to be abandoned as the player reverts to their familiar recourse of trying to get their technique right by searching for their swing.

HOW CAN YOU MINIMISE THE DEFAULT TENDENCY AT THIS LEVEL?

Stop putting the cart before the horse! Remember, the key to a connected swing is a quieter mind, one that can be more related to the body.

TRY THIS NO. 6
START FROM THE INSIDE

The golf swing can either be a fluid, powerful motion or a collection of individual positions. It's fluid when you're in flow and fragmented when you're out of sync. What shows up in the way you swing the club depends on where you're positioned in yourself, i.e. CFM or TMB.

If you hit a few poor shots, it's vital that you try not to abandon the foundations of **Connected Golf** and all that you've learned so far.

Using your own insights from TRY THIS No. 3 — A NEW LOOK AT YOUR PRACTICE SWINGS, notice when you are coming away from the principles of natural movement; this will include rushing your preparation, holding your breath throughout the swing, feeling unbalanced, gripping the club too tightly, trying to muscle through the ball and so forth.

As you get closer to the inner condition of relaxed readiness, your natural swing will return, so put your energy and attention there and not on overthinking your technique.

LEVEL THREE: CONNECTED GOLF

The highest level of golf performance perfectly illustrates the third Performance Paradox, which states, 'To obtain the desired outcome, focus on the process'.

The process here is the training and development of certain Performance Practices and the on-course application of the internal conditions of flow, from which natural movement ensues. Simply put, it's about quietening the mind, reducing feelings of nerves and anxiety and activating the experience of synced-up trust, similar to that experienced in reactive sports and the martial arts.

This level is usually stumbled upon by accident, resulting in the perfectly connected shot.

HOW IS THIS LEVEL COACHED?

This level is coached using the principles and practices in *Breathe Golf* and *Connected Golf*.

We look at how this can benefit your short game in my audio programme *Connected Putting: Harmonising Mind, Breathing and Movement on the Greens*.

These protocols are part of the **Chi Performance** methodology which helps to unite mind and body, mental game and technique by using traditional training from the martial arts and meditative traditions of the East specifically applied to golf and sports performance.

WHAT IS THIS LEVEL'S APPROACH TO PRACTICE?

These players understand that efforts made towards working on the mind-body connection of the operator of the golfer machine are as important as understanding the fundamentals of good swing mechanics.

This level is all about having a workable Performance Practice based on a methodology which encompasses the twin pillars of awareness of breathing and the principles of natural movement to ensure a measurable correlation between the time and effort spent practising and how that shows up on the course.

WHAT IS THIS LEVEL'S APPROACH TO PLAYING?

This feedback from a student perfectly illustrates this:

> *"I have loved working with Jayne on my breathing and becoming more aware of how my body is feeling on the golf course. I have come to the realisation that I don't need to interfere with what I am doing when I am in the zone; I don't need to start thinking or have a checklist of things I need to do like I have done in the past. When I am in the zone on the course, I can just let myself go and enjoy the moment, but when I do start to feel nervous or anxious over a shot, I now know a better way of helping me get back into the zone. When I feel nervous now, I just feel my breathing in the t'an tien and how my feet feel on the ground, and that helps me to get back to a calmer state where my mind and body can work together."*

Gemma Dryburgh, LPGA and LET professional player, Women and Golf tour ambassador

WHAT HAPPENS AT THIS LEVEL UNDER PRESSURE?

The player can generally override the default tendency by following their breathing, relaxing into the body, being aware of their inner conditions at set-up, taking their time and trusting that their natural swing will result from a more connected level of being.

We'll look more closely at this in Chapter Ten: The Connected Set-Up.

HOW CAN YOU MINIMISE THE DEFAULT TENDENCY AT THIS LEVEL?

Develop a Performance Practice; this can be done alongside taking lessons from your swing professional. It doesn't generally mix well with mental game strategies and quick fix mindfulness tips, although many students have come into this work after becoming interested in meditation from using an app on their smartphone.

TRY THIS NO. 7
GOLF PERFORMANCE MANTRA

One breath at a time, one shot at a time and one hole at a time.

CHAPTER SIX

TRANSFORMING YOUR GAME

"The way is in training."

Miyamoto Musashi

Connected golf, level three on our 'Performance Pyramid' depends on a player's ability to activate a state of *relaxed readiness* so characteristic of the zone or flow, particularly in the moments *before* they take their swing.

As we've seen, this state is characterised by a reduction of anxiety, a lack of mental interference, an alert relaxation, clarity of intent and a quiet confidence, which then manifests in what hundreds of players have called 'the effortless shot'.

Chances are you've already had this experience and have started to reflect upon this as we journey through the book together, shifting our perspective from movement to stillness and from thinking to quietening the mind.

The first steps in establishing the internal connections necessary to transform your game are, in fact, based on what you already know to be true. For instance, you've seen that when you examine the difference between your practice swing and taking the shot for real, you notice that what actually changes is taking place within you, the golfer. This then determines the quality of your swing and the delivery of the clubhead to the ball.

So making a start on this alternative paradigm isn't so much a leap of faith but more akin to the solid ground of your own experience when you no longer buy into many of the myths the mainstream perpetuates. Embracing this work is simply a question of trusting what you've already experienced, not what you've been told.

It begins with making the most effective use of your practice time, in an interesting and rewarding journey of self-exploration and discovery, undoing the cycle of diminishing returns and releasing your natural abilities.

Taking the first, simple steps towards developing more inner connectivity as you stand over the ball will bring untold rewards.

Slowing down a little, anchoring your attention in your physical body, noticing your breathing, feeling how your body responds to your intention and listening for signs that you're out of sync, not quite balanced or comfortable over the ball, all bring a level of transformation to the golfer that, in turn, transforms their game.

Ask yourself the following questions and make some notes in your journal:

1. **What resonates with you from Part One?** Maybe it's the tension you've noticed when you stand over the ball as opposed to when taking your practice swings. It might be seeing the tendency to default to searching for your swing rather than believing in your ability. It could be something very simple, like deciding not to try so hard and muscle your way through the ball.

2. **Write up all the things you can begin to practise now to start this transformational process.** This will include doing the TRY THIS exercises from Part One, especially the ones you can do regularly and in everyday life. You might also like to begin a daily meditation, quietening your mind with the learning from *Breathe Golf*.

3. **What can you stop doing right now in order to become the golfer you're meant to be?** This will include unplugging from the mainstream, foregoing all those tips and tricks videos on YouTube and the endless gathering of information. It will also mean refraining from fiddling with your swing during a round, relaxing a bit more, looking around you and taking in the natural world.

4. **Read through Part Two while transforming your approach to practice by doing/not doing the things you've decided upon.** Make a note of things that stand out for you, then go back and read it all again. Remember, this is a

complete paradigm shift which took over 30 years of training, research and coaching to figure out, so please take your time, be committed and methodical and give it a fair chance.

TRY THIS NO. 8
SOLO ROUND

Aim to play a solo round using what you've learned so far, particularly taking on board the things that resonate strongly for you and which you feel will make the biggest difference to your performance. Don't try everything at once; two or three simple keys maintained consistently over 18 holes will be most beneficial.

In this instance, you will score yourself on how well you stayed with your chosen supports and the quality of your inner state (where you are on the scale from CFM to TMB) in the moments before you take the shot. As Nicklaus said in his seminal book *Golf and Life*, the game is really one of self-mastery.

In Part Two, we're going to look more closely at the Eastern wisdom upon which **Connected Golf** is based and explore some very useful principles to help you execute more of those effortless shots; we'll start by setting a benchmark for connected movement itself.

PART TWO

CHAPTER SEVEN

SETTING A BENCHMARK

*"Finally, after thirty years,
someone understood."*

Japanese proverb

As we've seen from our study of the three levels of golf, it's important to acknowledge the underlying causes of poor performance so you can continue to recognise the need to overcome anxiety, overthinking and mentally searching for the perfect swing.

Too often, after a round, golfers will typically and persistently talk about the negative aspects of their swing action, errant drives and poor fairway shots without fully understanding or taking into account the fundamental reasons for this.

What should be a pleasant morning on the course so often turns into a source of frustration, but as we deepen our exploration of the principles of connected movement, and as you set about training these with the exercises in this book, you will have a greater understanding of how to fulfil your potential as a player. Consequently, you will enjoy golf a whole lot more.

Earlier, we touched upon the two pillars of *Connected Golf*, which have their origins in the martial and Zen arts of the Eastern world. Over the course of our journey together, we will look at these in more detail with the intention that they can become a new set of guiding principles to help you bring your mind and body into closer union. From this inner connection, your swing motion will naturally improve.

For ease of understanding, the two pillars are distilled into awareness of the breathing and awareness of the body, respectively. This is not to say that they are trained separately. For instance, when we follow the breath, the mind quietens down, and the body relaxes.

The two pillars include but are not limited to:

1. Practices to facilitate an expanded awareness of breathing, typically trained using formal meditation. The meditative state, so akin to the sporting zone and flow, is encouraged by observing the breath. As the breathing deepens and slows

down, analytical thinking, anxiety and nervous tension are reduced. In a performance situation, the applied meditative state helps complex movement to flow freely. This was fully explored in my book **Breathe Golf**.

2. Practices to facilitate an expanded awareness of the body and to develop the functional movements of the body according to causal principles that include both structure and relaxation. In a pressure situation, these principles are applied to help the body move freely and be a conduit for natural forces like leverage and rotation. This ensures the most efficient delivery of movement.

Eastern principles all spring from the central tenet of keeping the mind within the body, thus allowing thought and motion to complement each other and allow for the spontaneous release of physical action.

In this part, we're going to look at some key concepts from Tai Chi, which has often been called a meditation in motion. Tai chi, or Tai Chi Chuan to give its full title, translates as the 'supreme ultimate fist'. It is one of three so-called *internal* martial arts (Tai Chi, Hsing-Yi and Bagua) which sprang from the introduction of Kalaripayattu (an Indian martial art that dates back at least 3,000 years) and Yoga along with Chan Buddhism to China.

Legend states that in the 5th or 6th century, a Buddhist monk called Bodhidharma (Damo) travelled from India and began the physical training of the monks at the Shaolin Temple; these initial forms (Five Animal Frolics) later fused with Chinese culture and became kung-fu.

Chan later became widely known as Zen, the Japanese term for seated meditation, which uses the breath as the main focal point.

The concepts of Tai Chi are often conveyed in rather poetic language, and we'll examine them first in context before we see how they can be utilised for golf, both in the way that they can enhance or even replace what you're currently practising and in helping you take your range game onto the course.

Needless to say, as we're looking at principles and practices that served generations of warrior monks who often had to defend the temple from marauding invaders, these same exercises can certainly help your swing withstand the pressure of a golf tournament.

They will become your Performance Practices.

Before we start, it's important to understand that these concepts and their associated exercises and drills are not just another set of movements, nor are they a checklist. You don't have to memorise them, but through regular and persistent practice, the principles will become internalised or embedded into the *bodymind*; through training, we re-educate the physical body so that it will naturally respond to your intention for the shot, without CFM taking over to steer the movements.

I would advise you to read this part first before diving into the training in Part Three.

The foundational principle or concept is that of 'sung' or 'song', a Chinese word which means 'to relax without losing structure'; it is the benchmark principle that precedes all movement.

Sung is activated in stillness and applied when the body is in motion. It's one of the central qualities trained in the Standing Meditation (I Chuan or Zhan Zhuang) which will form the basis of your practice routine.

We've already started to explore how the condition of relaxed readiness, which includes sung as a core component, is the prerequisite inner state that allows mind and body to work together, such that movement will respond to and express your intention.

Sung includes a partial contraction of the musculature, which allows the practitioner to maintain their balance, central equilibrium and an upright posture. The image of the head being 'suspended' from above by a golden thread is an ancient instruction that enlivens the spirit and helps one to maintain a strong framework or posture while simultaneously relaxing. When working through these benchmark concepts, it's important to understand that the practitioner, by their efforts made in training, becomes positioned between two alternate states.

In sung, you are trying not to be completely relaxed but also not to be too stiff or rigid. Finding the space between is what's important; softness is required to produce power and speed, but without a supporting structure established by the body's skeleton and tendons, this softness can produce very little energy.

It's worth remembering here that all these ideas we're looking at are the result of instinctive and intuitive realisations given to the practitioner in a state of quiet contemplation.

In many cases, they were then honed, refined, tested and developed over successive generations, either of the same family or of the same school or lineage.

This is markedly different to the mass of analytically generated theories that abound in the golf industry today; in many cases, the excessive detail actually hinders players' attempts to move their bodies freely and play the game well.

Let's take a brief look at how you can begin to incorporate the qualities of sung into your golf set-up. You can think of it as a way to activate, enliven or switch on the body in order to prepare it for movement. It's an active relaxation like that of a cat or a snake ready to pounce.

There are four internal actions to master.

1. **Empty the chest**. Emptying or hollowing the chest is the first key to developing relaxed readiness as it softens the upper body, freeing the neck, releasing the shoulders and emptying the lungs. You'll find that exhaling deeply is a natural part of this process, which releases tightness and tension in the upper body.

2. **Engage the centre**. Lowering your awareness by bringing some of your attention to the navel area (t'an tien) creates more physical stability and helps you to breathe slowly and deeply. This, in turn, sends increased oxygen along with your 'feel-good' chemical signals (endorphins) to your brain. Please note, this is not a Pilates or core-strengthening exercise but something much more subtle that works on an energetic level. The centre naturally pulls in when the chest hollows.

3. **Load the legs**. Letting your upper body be supported by the muscles at the tops of the legs (psoas major) is the beginning of another crucial concept (that of 'opposing forces') which will have so many positive ramifications in your game. As you relax your shoulders, chest and arms and begin the process of becoming rooted in the lower body, you will be able to turn much more freely from the waist without compromising stability.

4. **Find the feet**. Running down the inside of your lower leg is the tibia or shin bone, the function of which is to support 90% of your body weight.

Positioning yourself on the front inside of your heels, just behind the instep, aligns you with the tibia and is the only place on the feet where you will be fully balanced and supported. The balls of the feet and the area behind the little toes are also important for anchoring to the ground, but the majority of the weight should be in the balance point.

Figure 5: The Balance Point

These internal actions complement and reinforce each other such that the more you empty the chest, the more you can be supported by the psoas and the more correctly you will be positioned on the feet thus increasing your ground force energy.

The muscles at the tops of the legs, centring on the inguinal crease (where your trousers crease when you're about to sit down), are called the 'kwa' in Tai Chi training. The importance of relaxing the upper body is so these muscles, which join the thigh to the torso, are engaged. This enhances lower body stability and will result in a more balanced golf swing with fewer moving parts.

Conversely, in the orthodox or mainstream approach to the set-up, few if any of these essential internal actions are acknowledged or adhered to.

Figure 6: Orthodox Set-Up – with the weight on the balls of the feet, the knees take the strain; there is little stability and the upper body is not fully supported by the legs

TRY THIS NO. 9
SUNG SET-UP

Set-up in your usual way, then set-up again using the four fundamental actions to activate sung *before* hinging at the hips to address the ball. In Chapter Ten, you'll find a unique set-up procedure that will include 'creasing the kwa', thus negating the tendency for the upper body to hang out in space as it tends to do using the mainstream set-up position.

For now, just compare the two postures and feel the increased load in the legs, which Hogan and Nicklaus, among others, have called the 'powerhouse' of the golf swing. If you have a golf buddy on hand, ask them to give you a gentle push in the sternum once you've set-up over the ball to see if they can unbalance you, first in your usual set-up and secondly when setting up more sung-style.

You'll most likely find that in the traditional set-up posture, there is very little stability, and you are easily pushed off balance, but in the sung set-up, your feet and legs really do provide 'a solid place to swing from' (Shivas Irons).

Figure 7: Connected Set-Up – applying the four fundamentals to activate 'sung' helps maintain a strong yet relaxed structure

From sung, we enter another huge concept from the Eastern martial arts, and that is 'peng'. This is best described as the bounce-back you'd feel if you punched a large rubber ball.

Peng takes sung and expands it into a taut but springy frame by gently pushing into the ground with the feet, along with an upwards or expansive motion of the spine. The opposite action is one of compression, where emptying the chest initiates a downwards movement into the ground. These actions are like a pulse that can be turned on and off. Compressing into the ground is what produces the power in a kung-fu punch; you only have to watch Bruce Lee prepare to strike his opponent to see how devastating this internal action can be.

When performing your golf swing, you can utilise peng from the moment you start moving.

From your take-away, this will include adhering to the four internal actions, i.e. keeping your chest empty, engaging your centre, feeling the upper body supported by the kwa and the balance points on the feet. At the top of your backswing, you can gently reinforce these inner actions, particularly emptying the chest so you can compress down, thus freeing the upper body to rotate while simultaneously gaining additional forward momentum.

Think of a rubber band stretched left and right to its maximum; when you let go of one side, the rubber band compresses of its own accord using the energy that was stored in the expansion. If you can create this feeling in your backswing, not only will you accelerate through the downswing, but the impact position will be true to your intention at set-up, and you will transfer more energy through the ball, which can be useful off the tee.

As my student, John K., who was living and working in Hong Kong at the time remarked,

> *"The impact Jayne's coaching has had on my game in only a few short weeks is more significant than the last three years of gym work, golf practice and competing on average five days per week... I have gained significant power and accuracy through the combination of breathing and controlling my biomechanics... as an over-40, to go from 100mph to 105mph in three years of working out to 112mph... is nothing short of incredible."*

Very often when golfers are at the top of their backswing, there is very little potential or stored energy left to initiate the transition. With a right-handed golfer, if the entire focus is towards the right side of the body, the position is not only unbalanced, but there is nothing in the left side to help initiate the downswing and release the club on its path.

Even if you do try for some separation at the top by simultaneously being in your opposite foot and leg, without awareness of peng this action can be forced and lack springiness. It is also very often accompanied by a tight and tense upper body in complete opposition to the principles of natural movement.

Please let me reiterate here that I am not a golf coach, nor do I play the game, and this has been a very deliberate decision that I've reaffirmed over the years, as I have always sought to present principles of movement rather than the technical aspects of golf. As you'll see in Chapter Nine, these principles of movement are equally applicable to every other sport.

Peng can be thought of as stretching the body's fascia or connective tissue without tensing the muscles. This is a fundamental skill that can be developed through training, sensitivity and feel. Without some looseness, the body will be too stiff. Without some tautness, the body can be too limp. Without stretching the two sides as well as front and back, the body is not properly connected; if the limbs and body are overextended, then they become too rigid. In all these cases, peng is lost.

Only with an understanding of this concept and the necessary training to develop such skills can the spiral motion taught by some of the world's top coaches actually be consistent with how the body naturally moves. Without peng, the tendency is for the upper and lower body to have the same qualities, which limits the function of the waist.

TRY THIS NO. 10
LIKE A PERFECTLY TENSIONED BOW

Ponder on this instruction from the legendary founder of Tai Chi, aiming to bring the qualities mentioned into your swing. When practising, you might like to go slowly and even pause at the top to feel the separation. Notice how the stretch increases the more you empty your chest.

> *"When you move upward, the mind must be aware of down;*
>
> *When moving forward, the mind also thinks of moving back;*
>
> *When shifting to the left side, the mind should simultaneously notice the right side — so that if the mind is going up, it is also going down".*
>
> **Attributed to Tai Chi Founder Chang San-feng,** ca. 1200 C.E.

Now, ask your golf buddy to provide some resistance by having them hold onto your wrists when you're at the top of your backswing. You'll notice immediately how natural movement instinctively takes over to perform your swing; with this additional weight, you have to initiate it with your lower body.

There is so much learning here, and, of course, your body has its own wisdom once you learn to listen, but here are some observations I've made about the usefulness of sung and peng in golf. As you start doing the training, you will gradually come to have insights of your own.

- The kinetic chain follows the same sequence no matter what the intended motion, as movement is always initiated from the ground and moves through the waist before transferring into the upper body. In Tai Chi training, we are taught that the upper body must *receive instruction* from the lower body before it starts to move. This is the case not just at golf's take-away but when transitioning from the top.

- Many golfers, even some of the world's elite, come up on the toes at impact in an attempt to deliver the maximum payload through the ball, but this could actually negate a lot of potential energy and also compromises balance, which can affect the trajectory of the ball. Emptying the chest at the top helps you compress your upper body so you can use the ground more efficiently at impact. This removes the necessity for standing on the toes. Instead, you will push the arches of the feet into the ground while allowing the coccyx to park itself horizontally, thus lengthening the spine.

- These actions conform to the principles of peng, creating a powerful yet elastic framework where the body can *transfer* rather than try to create leverage. The latter approach often leads to injuries and time away from the game.

- I've always felt uncomfortable about the term 'swing' as it implies a pendulum-like motion similar to that of my chiming clock, which has an equal and consistent momentum as it gently swings back and forth. I feel the movement made in golf is more like a strike or a kung-fu punch in that initially it requires the relaxed readiness of sung before turning into more of a coiled or sprung-loaded peng, which should naturally unwind of its own accord, right on target.

Here's a quick summary of the feedback from some of my students.

Learning to move the lower body first is helpful with lead and lag during the transition. I can shift my weight from one leg to the other without moving laterally.

I find that I can settle into my body more at address, which makes me feel calm yet powerful.

It's been great imagining the golf club as a weapon like a sword; it has been helping with the idea of storing and releasing energy at the right time.

Keeping my wrists soft helps to generate a whipping action which seems to happen by itself and stops me flicking my wrists.

Twisting and untwisting the waist helps the forearms to turn over naturally, and it's interesting that my hands at impact are bang opposite the t'an tien.

Everything feels more connected, especially the joints; there seems to be less independent movement. When one part of my body moves, all parts move, though the degree of movement of each part differs slightly. When I try to make this happen, it just doesn't work.

I relax my shoulders and arms completely when I address the ball and don't grip the club too tightly. I also concentrate on 'moving from the waist' and letting the club do the work. It's such an effortless feeling when it flies away right.

We'll examine all these concepts and more in the next chapter, paying particular attention to how they can help you bridge that all-important gap between practising your swing motion on the range and taking it to the course.

CHAPTER EIGHT

PRINCIPLES OF NATURAL MOVEMENT

"Man moves horizontally, but his primary relationship is downward. We forget that the power of the earth is an up-and-down function, and if not for that, no movement would be possible! Horizontal movement gives us freedom, but downward movement gives us power and stability."

Peter Ralston

In the Introduction, I mentioned how, upon hearing Jack Nicklaus' comment that 'golf is played with the feet', my life was steered in a particular direction, the culmination of which you're reading now.

I became fascinated with the possible synergy between golf and Tai Chi as the Golden Bear's remarks echoed that of the Tai Chi Classics, which state that movement begins in the feet, is issued through the legs, controlled by the waist and expressed in the hands.

Over the past decade, while working on the manuscript, Nicklaus has been my go-to model for learning about the game and understanding the key components of the golf swing. I believe he's the greatest player of all time and certainly the most consistent, very likely because he took his time at set-up as well as during the take-away, especially the more explosive or powerful the shot had to be. He was also famous for leaving his footprints in the ground after teeing off.

Nicklaus has said many times that the set-up is key and that if the golfer sets up well then, even if the swing isn't so good, the shot will still be the best it can be, but if the set-up is rushed then even if the swing motion is good, it will lack a proper foundation and consequently the shot will be poor.

This perfectly echoes the principles of natural movement, as we'll see.

Along with Nicklaus, I've also studied the archetypal swing of Ben Hogan, whose slow motion swing helped him to really feel how power comes from the ground, the burning intensity of Seve Ballesteros, the sheer athleticism of modern players like Brooks Koepka and Henrik Stenson and, (of course) the genius of Tiger Woods, known to be an avid meditator and Tai Chi practitioner in his youth.

In the women's game, I've appreciated the beautifully balanced separation and rhythm of the late, great Mickey Wright, along with the dynamic power of Laura Davies. In the modern game, I admire players like Brooke Henderson and Danielle Kang with their minimal leg action, subtle weight shift and unwinding of the lower body to start the downswing.

It's interesting that Kang was a martial arts practitioner for many years before becoming a natural talent in the game; she made history by qualifying for the US Open at the age of 14.

You probably have your own favourites, and it's possible you've started mentally criticising the swings of the older generation players I've mentioned, preferring the modern golf swing to the 'old-fashioned' swing of yesteryear.

Or you might prefer the classic swing, especially the lower body action which winds and unwinds to create a 'lag', leaving the clubhead behind, as opposed to the twisting of the back against the minimal leg and hip movement of today's players who use physical strength to close the clubface using the wrists and hands.

Whatever your preference, I'm sure you'll agree that, unfortunately, however great today's players might be from time to time, they lack consistency. It seems when the elite tee up, it's anybody's tournament, and a major win is often succeeded by years in the wilderness or at the very least missing the cut in the next event.

I'm sure you'll also agree that, since the advent and indeed explosion of technical instruction and information, players' games don't seem to have got any better when it comes to being able to perform under pressure. As Adam Scott's father Phil wrote in his commentary to my earlier book *Breathe Golf*, "In spite of the unprecedented improvements in knowledge of teachers and coaches within the industry, and the tools to impart this knowledge, improvement has proven elusive."

So rather than arguing back and forth as to whether the classic swing or the modern swing is best, I'd like to bring a third factor into the equation, and that is the connected swing.

As we've seen, it doesn't matter how much you know about swing mechanics, how many hours you spend practising or even what equipment you use; it's all about where you are on the scale from CFM to TMB when standing over those shots that really matter.

What I find extraordinary in golf and sports, *per se*, is the fact that players are led to believe that they can somehow organise the kinetic chain themselves by working to a particular technical formula and that they can encourage fluidity of movement by thinking through technique during a game.

Yet, as we're discovering, when you adhere to the fundamental laws of movement, your own natural swing will emerge; this allows for more consistency, as well as for individual physical differences and constraints, which lessens time spent away from the course due to injury.

Remember, **Connected Golf** is about the bringing together of the mind and body in order to lay the groundwork for flow to manifest itself and enhance the connection of your movement. This is not simply philosophy but a method or way to practise what's most important if you intend to deliver the complex motion of the golf swing in a way that's fluid yet precise under pressure.

This is markedly different to golf psychologists who promote the idea that 'the body can self-organise around an idea'. It may be true when the player is in flow, but the body *cannot* organise itself around an idea that is too prominent and which activates the analytical mind, nor can it self-organise if the athlete's biochemistry isn't under control and they have switched into the stress-response.

I hope the training in this book will put an end to this disparity and clearly demonstrate the right internal conditions needed by the athlete in order to intuitively deliver their intent.

We're now going to explore some traditional Tai Chi concepts that can help you put together your own connected swing; these are embodied in key phrases or sayings that have been passed down over the centuries. You could think of them, as one of my teachers said, as 'big ideas' to ponder on; try to understand them and slowly integrate them into your golf game.

We will look at these concepts in and of themselves before using them as a set of guidelines or parameters that can support your swing. In the final part of the book, you'll find the means to train them so they can become the foundations for helping you bridge the gap between practice and the course and move up through the three levels of performance identified in Chapter Five.

Don't rush or try to do too much at once; just work with two or three principles that most resonate with you next time you tee it up.

This is about re-educating the frenetic, modern body, which is always mind-led and very often top-heavy. What I mean is that in most people, the breath is shallow in the upper chest, the shoulders are tight and raised and the centre of gravity is shifted from its rightful place below the navel to the area of the sternum. In addition to this, the psychological space has taken precedence over awareness of the physical self or the environment.

The exercises in Part Three might seem simple enough, but that shouldn't suggest they are easy. The training is given just as it is in traditional martial arts to help you reverse the unnatural polarity symptomatic of modern life and bring the energy and the attention down into the lower body so that movement can be initiated from the ground.

You will be doing the same few exercises day in and day out, over many weeks and months, learning to move from the bottom to the top rather than head-first. In Tai Chi, this takes many years to accomplish, but luckily I've spent a couple of decades working out the exact principles and drills which will help you train the right kind of strength and inner connection for a relaxed yet powerful golf swing.

Consistent training is the key. Your synced-up *bodymind* knows what to do, and **Connected Golf** is the antidote to all those menus of movement positions that fill your head when you're standing over the ball.

STILLNESS IS THE MASTER OF MOTION

This is a classic Tai Chi phrase which is echoed in the latest evidence from those who've been studying the brainwaves of world-class and Olympic athletes for over three decades.

Neuroscientists have come to the same conclusion, and it's been neatly and succinctly expressed by Steven Yellin as 'the quality of the gap, determines the quality of the motion' in his book *The 7 Secrets of World Class Athletes*.

The researchers have proven that the athlete with the quietest mind in the moments before throwing, kicking or striking a ball in a competitive situation is always the one who delivers the most fluid and precise motion.

Many of the greatest golfers have spoken of their personal experience with silence and stillness: from Bobby Jones, who said that when he played good golf, he thought very little, and when he played great golf, he didn't think at all, to Tiger Woods reflecting that he heard nothing, no thoughts at all, in the moments before hitting some of his most creative and iconic shots.

STAND LIKE A MOUNTAIN, MOVE LIKE A RIVER

This is another well-known phrase from Tai Chi that helps us understand that in order to move most efficiently, the upper and lower body must have different or opposing qualities which are 'resolved' through the waist. These are explained as Yang or positive, strong and forceful energy and Yin or negative, soft and yielding energy, respectively.

This means that the lower body (yang/mountain) is strong and stable, while the upper body (yin/river) is loose and free of tension. These conflicting forces are harmonised through the body's physical centre, the t'an tien, which lies approximately two inches below the navel.

Consequently, the upper and lower body never move in sequence; action is intended by the mind (Yi), which then initiates movement from the feet, before transferring it through the waist and into the upper body.

We see this sequence so clearly in the classic golf swing, particularly the lag in transition, as the lower body is already coming back when the hands are at the top, creating what looks like a slight pause before the upper body follows the impetus created by the hips, waist and weight transfer in the lower body.

We also see this action very much in the women's game, as women can naturally distinguish between their hips and waist when they move. The body motion of some of today's greats from South Korea, like Inbee Park and Jeongeun Lee ('Lucky 6') epitomise this phrase.

ROOTED IN THE FEET, SPRINGING FROM THE LEGS, MOVING THROUGH THE WAIST AND EXPRESSED IN THE HANDS

This principle sums up the laws of natural movement; it is the perfect description of escalation or the kinetic chain (to use phrases from biomechanics), and it applies to all sporting movement, all of the time.

In the mainstream approach to coaching golf technique and swing positions, results are often counter to what's intended. This is especially true when the golfer is encouraged to deliberately think through and piece together the kinetic chain without being shown how to initiate that movement naturally by utilising balance, true relaxation and the centre of gravity.

Moreover, these fundamental laws of movement get hijacked by overthinking and the determination to 'get it right', instead of letting the body do what it wants to do naturally.

The analytical mind gets in the way by trying to force things, and anxiety disrupts the biochemistry so that the body gets tight and stiff. Therefore, it becomes difficult to transition well from the top if the breathing and centre of gravity remain up in the chest, no matter how strong the legs are from doing all those squats in the gym.

FINDING YOUR CENTRE

To find your physical centre, relax the muscles, joints and tendons while maintaining an upright posture. Feel as if your head is suspended from above, and your feet are supported from below.

As the body relaxes, you can feel the weight of the upper body emptying down into the legs and feet due to the law of gravity. You will feel a subtle shift downwards as your centre of gravity slightly lowers. Avoiding upper body fullness, you will feel your breathing, chest and shoulders sinking towards the navel area, which helps ensure the physical centre stays in the lower t'an tien (dantien). Through the standing meditation the physical centre can be developed so that your connection to the ground is more stable. With the silk reeling (moving the centre) and other exercises (see Part Three), it can become the initiation point for movement itself. When moving from the centre, both the take-away and the plane or angle of approach take care of themselves, and you won't have to keep checking during the swing.

As the mind settles to the centre, calm and stillness are created. It's the first step to becoming more connected. When you start overthinking and trying too hard, excess tension is created, which stops the body obeying this natural force.

Figure 8: Rotating Around the Centre – using the t'an tien as the pivot-point of motion

MOVING THE CENTRE

In the early Tai Chi classes I attended in the late 1980s and early 1990s, students were initially taught a number of separate movements with exotic names like 'holding the ball', 'ward off', 'play the lute', 'crane spreads wings' and 'carry tiger to mountain'.

Over successive months and years of training, these individual movements became joined together by using the intention mind (Yi) and the t'an tien as ways to coordinate the initially compartmentalised movements into a seamless whole.

What's so useful about using the t'an tien as an idea in golf is that it helps us visualise and produce movement in three dimensions. This is, of course, intended through analysis of swing planes, but without a pivot-point around which to swing, this motion is difficult for many golfers to grasp and reproduce. It's unfortunate and largely unnecessary that so many amateur golfers flail their arms around arbitrarily, trying to produce a consistent swing motion without them having any meaningful connection to the body.

In Tai Chi, the practitioner moves around an imaginary centre which Grandmaster Yang Chen Fu (Yeung Chengfu) calls 'the commander of the body' in his 10 Essential Points for Tai Chi Chuan.

To help, picture a golf ball positioned inside the lower body, two finger widths underneath the navel and two-thirds of the way from front to back so that it sits just in front of the spine.

It's a great sensory aid for helping you accelerate through the ball as the centre of the body can spin faster and more efficiently than the clumsy rotation often initiated by the chest and shoulders, which especially seems to happen in times of pressure.

The inimitable golf coach John Jacobs wrote about how 'the inside of the body moves the outside', and with the ball-like t'an tien as the fulcrum of motion, functioning like the hub of a wheel, it's easy to see how the path of the golf club traces the outside of this wheel while staying fundamentally connected to the body.

SPIRAL ENERGY (SILK REELING)

Spiral energy is a curve in three dimensions. You can imagine it like a corkscrew thread which compresses or contracts into the ground before expanding upwards and outwards.

It has traditionally been taught and developed in the martial arts through the use of 'silk reeling' exercises or *chan ssu jin*, the idea being that one must move as if drawing silken thread from a cocoon, without breaking or snapping the thread.

This intention allows the energy to spiral upwards from the ground and move through the waist, which, in turn, enables the levers or joints of the arms (shoulder, elbow and wrist) to open and close naturally. The exercises train the body to move as one unit, led by the t'an tien.

I often advise my students to gently spiral the knees outwards at set-up (similar to how the early Wing Chun practitioners would stabilise their Siu Lim Tao form), which assists in anchoring the lower part of the legs to the ground. It's important that this is done correctly and should, in fact, be a strong idea or intention that the body obeys. Of course, one needs to train stillness and mental quietude in order for the subtlety of these internal actions to be felt.

Let the hips turn 45 degrees from the front with a slow take-away and when the hips have reached this angle, allow the waist to continue turning. The conflict that is created between the energies of the lower and upper body, as a result, helps create maximum torque, which should not be easy to hold at the top. Your body will then unwind naturally and sequentially from the ground through the waist, culminating in a natural opening of the elbow and turn of the wrists as they pass the body's centre.

Paying attention to these key points will help your upper body stay just behind the movement of your lower body from the top, with the arms and consequently the clubhead unwinding on plane.

I am particularly reminded of the unconventional swing of Jim Furyk and the spiral or curved looping motion made at the top, which is so reminiscent of this.

Without an understanding of the model of human movement that we get from the martial arts and which includes ground connection and waist connection, drills that deliberately encourage a spiral-like motion, however innovative, can miss vital components.

In particular, if the golfer is taught to set-up on the balls of the feet, the rest of the body will have to compensate for this infraction of natural movement principles, and it will throw off sequential areas of support like the muscles at the tops of the legs, which should correspond to the balance point on the feet. It might work well on the practice ground but can be difficult to maintain under pressure.

In Part Three, you'll find the drills to help train the *feeling* of spiral motion or escalation so that you can refrain from holding yet another set of instructions in your mind while taking your shot. Building a stronger base, more relaxation in your torso and arms, and the ability to move from the body's centre will help initiate and release the kinetic chain naturally, without you having to think about it.

TRY THIS NO. 11
DRAWING A FIGURE OF EIGHT

Start by holding the club in front of you, parallel to the ground, opposite the chest.

To begin the figure of eight movement, the clubhead will first pass behind your left shoulder and down to your left hip, then travel up the centre line to its starting position before passing behind your right shoulder, down past your right hip and up the centre line again.

At first, you'll want to use your arms and wrists, but if you can relax your shoulders and settle down into the legs, you'll be able to bring some movement into your waist and begin to activate the t'an tien. You will then feel how the motion of the t'an tien influences the wrists to turn more freely.

As you continue, the more relaxed your upper body and the more stable your legs are, the faster you'll propel the club. If it's too tough on your wrists holding the shaft, then hold the clubhead to perform the drill.

Aim to make ten repetitions starting from your left side and ten starting from the right.

Many coaches suggest players make a deliberate wrist hinge at set-up, which will be held in place until impact; however, from the above exercise and all you're learning about fundamental movement principles, you'll agree that in some cases, this can hinder freedom of movement, restricting the natural impetus of the centre of gravity and can make the body very stiff and unresponsive.

Add pressure to the equation, and you're back to searching for a swing.

You'll often get much better results on the course if you simply maintain the balance points throughout your swing and let escalation occur naturally. The wrists and hands don't create leverage but should *express* the spiral energy issuing from the feet and t'an tien.

You can imagine the t'an tien as a trackball that moves around in response to the spiral force generated at your feet. It's not something you have to make happen, as it occurs naturally when the body is allowed to move the way it wants to.

SINK THE SHOULDERS

Although we touched on this earlier, it's worth repeating, and indeed, in Yang Chen Fu's 10 essentials of Tai Chi, he twice mentions the imperative of setting the shoulders down. This is important for a number of reasons, not least of which is that when the shoulders are raised, both the breathing and the centre of gravity rise up higher in the body, negating power and strength and compromising the potential connectedness of movement.

As an LPGA coach remarked when attending one of my workshops, if the shoulders are raised, the breathing and energy are most likely concentrated in the chest; the chest will therefore tend to lead the downswing, causing an outside-in swing path which can result in topping the ball.

With the increasing self-awareness you'll develop following the drills, exercises and principles in this book, you'll be able to ensure the shoulders stay down for the duration of your shot. Sinking or loosening the shoulders at set-up and again at transition encourages the chest to sink in turn, helping you harness both the physical centre and the ground for increased precision and power in your ball-striking.

INTERNAL STRENGTH

Connected Golf is simplified golf; you don't need to memorise positions or learn a lot of coordinated movement, but instead, change the emphasis of your practice to develop the correct structure of the body, which, in turn, will move the load, i.e. the golf ball. In this way, there will be fewer moving parts to your swing.

Once you know how to balance properly, you'll feel the difference this creates to your take-away, backswing, downswing, moment of impact, follow-through and finish position. In the simplest terms, a connected swing is one where stability, strength, and, therefore, resistance is created with the lower body, while the upper body relaxes into and is supported by the legs. The physical centre of gravity is utilised to create coil, allowing the upper body to follow or respond to the impetus created by the lower body (in both the classic and modern variants). As such, the elbows and wrists will hinge and unhinge as a direct consequence of moving the centre, which, in turn, responds to the balance points on the feet, the psoas and the other muscles at the tops of the legs.

Maintaining these parameters while moving helps ensure that your golf swing will start and finish on the same plane. This is the most natural path of movement your body can take; it's the way it wants to move and does move when all that mental interference and anxiety is put to one side.

Understanding and utilising these principles, which we've taken from Tai Chi and which are echoed in other similar arts such as Japan's Aikido and Judo, demonstrate how posture and gravity complement each other to create whole-body motion, as opposed to moving isolated parts in a deliberately choreographed sequence.

Central to this form of relaxed power is the resolution of opposites; upright force comes from the ground, while vertical force is generated by emptying the chest, setting the shoulders down and compressing or loosening down into the feet.

The body can then rotate freely in a horizontal plane while the arms simultaneously move on the vertical plane. These internal actions and opposing forces are all united in the body's centre of gravity, which, as we've seen, is the one true pivot-point.

All the training in this book is designed to help you develop the inner connections that enable the body to move in the most efficient way, even under pressure. When you no longer have to worry about swing thoughts and individual moving parts, your mental attention is freed-up and better employed for intention and visualisation purposes.

ENERGY IN MOTION

Some years ago, I was coaching at the K Club in Ireland, and a student told me he'd had the good fortune to be seated next to Tiger Woods at a dinner there and had enjoyed an enlightening conversation with him about the game. According to Woods, the number one mistake made by competitive amateurs is that of the 'grip it and rip it' approach, thinking that the harder they swing, the better. In fact, the opposite is true, and even more crucially, from the standpoint of the Eastern practices you're learning, a balanced and rooted set-up coupled with the relaxation of the upper body enlivens the whole body and creates a more whip-like energy through the ball.

Moreover, you're hopefully beginning to realise the power of intention, which can only be employed once overthinking is put to one side. The Chinese martial arts look in such detail at this subject, stating that first the idea or intent occurs, and then the energy in the body responds to this idea, activating it for movement before the physical body itself is called to action. We'll examine this fascinating link between intention and movement in the next chapter.

The list of concepts covered so far is by no means definitive and we will carry on exploring the inner and outer conditions necessary for connected movement throughout the rest of the book. For now, let's hear more from my students about their experience of working with these principles in their golf practice and playing.

"Overall, the routine, process and breathing helps me calm my mind, forget about technical thoughts and allows me to flow better through my swing. I can sense more effortless power, and this encourages me to trust my swing and ability. I already feel more stable, calmer and controlled and am thinking of returning to competitions."

Andy W. PGA coach

"I have practised your drills most days of the week for around half an hour each time and have envisioned my success. During the actual matches, I just monitored my mind-body connection, enjoyed the company and encouraged my partner while focusing on the target. In spite of the pressure, I never once felt anything but comfortable and confident. I am now known for being a very strong finisher."

J.K. Hong Kong

"When I try to create a good swing tempo, it doesn't work, and it feels like I'm forcing it and giving myself yet another thing to think about, but when I work on being in my breathing and the balance point on the feet, my swing rhythm seems to take care of itself."

John H. Surrey

"A few months ago, I started paying more attention to 'the benefits of stillness' and having a strong base. Once I had spent some time on this and practising breathing in just before my backswing and releasing through the swing, I found my drives going straighter and longer all through the round. For the past half a dozen rounds, everyone I play with has commented on it, and I have been setting up opportunities in competitions."

Doug H. Edinburgh

"I have always believed there is a connection between the posture and movement in the martial arts and the golf swing. Your Standing Meditation is helping to improve my structure and also gives me the ability to feel more rooted at address and use my core better. I also feel like I have more forward drive through impact."

Matt C. PGA coach

"I find when I'm overthinking the shot, my movements tend to be jerky, but if I can stay with feeling that my mind, body and breathing are somehow connected in the t'an tien, the wrists turn over naturally, creating better contact with the ball."

Howie K. California

One of the biggest difficulties with the golf swing is the tendency to see it as an unnatural movement requiring ongoing specialist instruction, but as we're going to see in the next chapter, the principles we're looking at apply equally well to other sports and consequently could help make your route to becoming a better player so much simpler and more enjoyable.

When we bring fundamental movement skills rather than just technique into our exploration of golf, we will see that they are immediately applicable and that, in fact, you already know most of them from everyday movements, and they might also be embedded from your other sports or fitness pursuits. For instance, if you play tennis, baseball, hockey or tenpin bowling, you might already have the skills necessary to elevate your golf. You will certainly have learned something about balance, rotation, joint-stacking, the kinetic chain and so forth. It's all a question of transferring these into your game.

CHAPTER NINE

TRANSFERRING SKILLS FROM OTHER SPORTS

"I can teach many sports, but, obviously, tennis is the one. When you do other sports, you see things from different perspectives: different footwork drills, body positions, angles and geometry. All that stuff is helpful, and so when I do other sports, I can see things because once you know one sport, then the other sport becomes clearer."

Martina Navratilova

I'm a big fan of Martina and have heard her say several times that a true athlete should be able to turn their hand to any sport, and, as one of the greatest tennis players of all time, she's got a fantastic golf swing to prove her point! Interestingly, after golfers, my second biggest client base is tennis players, to whom I teach the same principles of natural movement that you're learning in *Connected Golf*.

These principles constitute the practice necessary for high-performance in any sport, i.e. the procedures and processes necessary to seamlessly deliver complex movement against other athletes of equal ability in competitive situations.

In fact, they supplement and support technical and mental game skills in practice and preparation but take precedence when you need to perform under pressure.

Working with athletes from many different sports, it's been remarkable to see that very often the transference of ability from one sport to another is actually the transference of fundamental movement skills.

Or at least, it should be.

Most, if not all, sports are simply fundamental movements which employ the use of natural forces that exist in the universe and within the human body: things like balance, torque or spin, and leverage; many even work (and play) directly with gravity such as in skiing, slacklining, free climbing and parkour.

What's exciting for the spectator and challenging for the contestants is that these complex movements have to be released against others of the same technical, physical and mental abilities in front of a crowd and often a worldwide audience tuning in on television or social media.

Coming back to ball sports, it seems that golf, more than tennis, cricket, baseball, soccer, hurling, hockey, tenpin bowling or any other game you mention that involves throwing, kicking or hitting a ball with a bat, club or racket, complicates the hell out of what should be a fairly natural movement.

As Bruce Lee wrote in his book *The Art of Expressing the Human Body*, there are only so many things the body can do, i.e. if I extend my arm with my palm upwards and contract the bicep muscle, my arm will bend or hinge inwards from the elbow; my arm will not bend or fold outwards, so there are only a certain amount of functional movements that the body can display, and we cannot work outside these parameters.

In golf, the current paradigm of coaching the body (technique) and the mind (mental game and psychology) separately exacerbates the inherent mind-body split we looked at in Chapter Two. It's the same across all sports but has been taken to the point of diminishing returns in golf.

The golf swing has been written about more than any other sporting motion, but the mistaken assumption that's held even at the highest echelons of the game, which then filters down to the grassroots player, is that swing theory converts to performance potential. It doesn't. How can it when explanations of swing technique can include anywhere up to 100 individual positions that the golfer is expected to memorise and recreate by recalling them in the mind?

Swing theory is not golf; it's just ideas about movement, not the reality of how things are in a moment of play, especially when under pressure. Standing over the ball, thinking about the technique you're going to perform in a few moment's time, nullifies the mind-body connection and activates the analytical mind, which then captures the signal intended for the motor system and results in a clumsy execution of movement and a wayward ball.

I believe everybody knows this, but, like the elephant in the room, it isn't acknowledged, and because nobody from golf has posited a solution to the paradox of performance, the same theories are regurgitated over and over.

It's time to look at golf differently, and perhaps, coming from outside the industry, I can help you do just that.

I propose that the golf swing is an athletic movement similar to existing sporting movements, but the link between intent and action has been all but cancelled out in the modern era due to the insistence on overthinking and the deliberate steering of the body into certain positions.

The golfer is taught to rely on their mind alone, whether it's thinking about their movement sequence or thinking about how they are thinking. Usually both!

I don't know the statistics on this, but my instinct tells me that in Nicklaus' era, fewer players choked or saw their games dramatically collapse due to pressure, whether that was crowd expectation, returning to their home course, or trying to get over a water hazard on the final day of a major.

With all the technological advances in equipment and the amount of time tour professionals spend working on their games, it's shocking the way they can crash out of a tournament after a disastrous first round or start double-bogeying on the back nine on a Sunday, squandering their lead over the rest of the field. We certainly don't see this type of thing happening so much in other sports. Can you imagine Roger Federer or Serena Williams double-faulting through the entire first set at Wimbledon?

So what is it about golf that makes it so difficult to transfer the movement of the swing from the range to the tee, even for players who know everything there is to know about technique and have all the money in the world to hire the best swing coaches, psychologists and mind coaches? Perhaps that's the problem!

A PGA coach I'm working with recently told me he isn't very good with technology and consequently couldn't work out how to give a detailed computer analysis of his clients' swings after every shot, so he ended up using the same image which had frozen on his home screen. After giving a few lessons like this, he had the unhappy realisation that all most golfers want is information, facts and figures, statistics and percentages. Even when they hit a left to right shot and the image showed a straight drive, they didn't see any disparity but still wanted their analytical mind to be satisfied with details about the swing plane, the arc of the ball and so forth.

This is the way the coaching industry is going, and along with the division of what should be a fairly flowing motion ('Two turns and a swish' according to John Jacobs) into a sequence of static, choreographed postures, it simply encourages the CFM to run rampant. On the course, this creates a tremendous amount of anxiety associated with trying to get it right and completely inhibits whole-body connection and fluidity of movement.

We've already seen how nerves, anxiety and mental interference wreak havoc with movement, aggravated by the fact that players are led to believe that analytical thinking, so helpful when honing technique, game strategy and course management, can improve their shot-making.

What it actually does is disrupt the link between your intention for the shot and how your body wants to move in order to carry out that intention.

As mentioned earlier, you don't have to force the kinetic chain, muscle through the ball or try to enhance leverage; just put the foundations of movement in place that will allow the body to respond most efficiently and naturally to your intention. As you develop your Performance Practice, you'll be doing this with the help of the TRY THIS exercises as well as the Standing Meditation, silk reeling and other associated exercises in Part Three: Training and Drills.

With the foundations of movement in place, your own natural swing becomes locked within a strong yet pliable structure (remember sung?) that can support a complexity and subtlety which the mind simply cannot grasp; without them, it becomes a controlled mistake which invariably comes undone once the pressure mounts.

As we touched upon briefly in the last chapter, athletic intent determines (or should determine) the position of the body, and this includes how and from where movement is initiated or triggered. We see this quite clearly in reactive sports (i.e. when the athlete is responding to a moving ball or target). Watching the baseball at Tokyo 2020, it was beautiful to see the swings initiating from the legs and hips before transferring through the waist and into the arms in an instinctive and natural reaction to the pitch.

You might argue that it's different in golf as the player has a static rather than moving ball to hit, although just looking at the spirit of intent in the eyes of the late, great Seve Ballesteros and his body position at impact dispels this belief.

Closer to golf, other sports that begin from relative stillness like shooting and archery also consist of a reaction to intent in the same way as reactive sports, and much has been written about how these sports utilise inner stillness, posture and breathing to summon TMB.

For instance, in one of my favourite books, *Kyudo, The Art of Zen Archery* by Hans Joachim Stein, the emphasis on establishing a balance between mind and body is seen as imperative and the term yugamae is used to describe this state of being prepared to release the arrow.

"The *yugamae* also needs to be practised by focusing on the physical and spiritual centre, the tanden, without deliberation but with full and undivided concentration. The manipulations constituting the *yugamae* will then be initiated by the lower abdomen instead of arising in the hands themselves. Hands and arms are then only executing the impulses which – although coming from the brain – only find concrete expression in the lower abdomen. Once the archer has made these motions automatic, to such an extent that they 'flow' from his inner centre without the deliberate participation of his will, the spectator will gain the impression that movements during the *yugamae* arise of their own accord and have a life of their own, taking its substance from the archer's centre."

When the mind is that bit quieter, intention and action are closer. It's that synced-up feeling of trust on the deepest level.

So, what exactly is intention?

In the modern age, we've all but made a god of the analytical mind, and rather than allowing it to function as it should for analysing information, organising tasks and solving problems, we tend to use it for everything, even tasks it wasn't designed for. In golf and sports, intention and its allied function visualisation are believed to be a part of analytical thinking, but this is a very limited and restrictive view.

The Tai Chi masters of antiquity demonstrated that real intent actually determines the position of the body, i.e. how it's primed or triggered for movement, but this understanding, like most of Eastern wisdom, has been watered down into palatable mental game theories which don't require what I'd consider to be deep or purposeful practice.

Here's what I wrote about intention in my eBook, ***The Practice of High-Performance***.

"Any fault that shows up in your movement routine or sequence, whether it's mistiming, lack of tempo, loss of balance or you're way off target, all begins with a lack of sync between mind and body at set-up. Instead of stillness and intention, your mind gets busy thinking about the movement you're going to perform and detaches itself from the body and the breathing, going off into its own little world imagining it can influence movement.

"Simply put, if you don't try too hard to control your movements, especially if they are embedded through repetition and practice, you only need to *get out of the way* and allow them to be released quite naturally.

"Intention (Yi) primes the body for movement and results in a chain of events which could be summed up in three words: idea – activation – movement, and so long as this sequence or natural circuit is not interrupted or broken by analytical thinking, your movement will flow.

"If you notice any signs that you're interfering with this sequence, if you're nervous, anxious or thinking too much, step aside and regroup before taking your shot or performing your routine.

"The athlete's role is to lay the ground for mind and body to work together without trying too hard to make it happen. A higher level of intense concentration is needed but one that is not attached to the result but stays in the moment."

It's my belief that **Connected Golf** can help you simplify your swing into fewer moving parts, locked within certain key areas of the body which support balance, rotation, vertical force and so on, such that your own natural swing can become a reaction to your intention about where you want the ball to land.

Of course, an understanding of ball flight laws, including position at set-up, also contributes to summoning your intent for the shot, and we'll explore this more in the following chapters.

For the moment, let's look a bit closer at how all sporting motions can be summoned through the triad of 'idea, activation and movement' in the same way as the martial arts. We'll do this with the help of a couple of TRY THIS exercises, which will serve to demonstrate how the body instinctively responds to a clear idea, especially when this idea is supported by a relaxed attention and within a stable yet pliable physical structure.

First, we're going to look at a simple athletic exercise you might have done at the gym, and then we'll look at a move from the martial arts to demonstrate that you already know much of what I'm talking about and have had the direct experience that you can instinctively allow your body to move the way it wants to, without the necessity to think too much about it.

You only have to imagine striking a baseball pitch, releasing a bowling ball or playing a backhand cross court pass and your body automatically responds with the neurons and muscle fibres reacting in the way they would if you were performing the movement for real. This is why visualisation, or more correctly, visual motor rehearsal, is used by so many elite athletes, but again, we're going to look at this phenomenon not from a mental game perspective but from this new paradigm of the mind-body connection.

We'll pay particular attention to the process used by Jack Nicklaus and the latest research, which gives credence to the Golden Bear's instincts about how this process can most positively influence the shot. Every shot Nicklaus hit, whether on the practice area or on the course, had a purpose and intention behind it, and in the days before the explosion of technical and psychological theories, Nicklaus' mind was quiet yet focused enough to touch on something quite extraordinary.

What all movement in golf, sport and life comes down to has been encapsulated in the Tai Chi concepts we looked at earlier; it's all a matter of weight shift, rotation through the waist and delivery through the upper body. These movements can occur naturally and in the right sequence if you get out of your own way. The following two exercises will clearly demonstrate this and help you find that essential feeling in your swing.

TRY THIS NO. 12
BALL SLAMMING

You can test this principle first by slamming a ball of different weights into the ground from just above your shoulder. You will notice how your body responds differently depending on the weight of the ball used.

To begin, stand with your feet shoulder-width apart, weight evenly distributed. Hold a fairly large but light ball like a beach ball between your hands in front of your waist. Turn your waist to your right, letting the hands move up to just above your shoulders. Now slam the ball into the ground between your feet. You should feel how the waist moves and how the hands come down naturally to their starting point. You can also try doing the exercise on the other side of the body, i.e. starting from the left.

Next, hold a slightly heavier ball like a football and do the same exercise on each side of the body. This time you'll notice the feeling of ground pressure in your right foot as you turn to the right and a slight emptying of the chest as you prepare to slam the ball.

Repeat each exercise several times, at normal speed, slowly and with your eyes closed to really get the feeling and awareness of what your body is doing.

Finally, pick up a heavy ball like an 8kg medicine ball and do the exercise again. This time notice how your body automatically and instinctively responds as the load is increased by bending the knees, lowering the centre of gravity, emptying the chest, applying ground force through the legs and releasing through the waist. You don't have to think about these things; they just happen.

For this exercise, you've simply repeated the same action but paid attention to how your body prepares itself for the varying forces by changing how far the knees are bent, how much to load the leg or tighten the core and so forth. You'll also notice that the idea or intention to slam the ball is perhaps accompanied by a visual image to which the body can react.

You could now practise a few slow motion swings holding the same intention that the structure of the body remains intact throughout the motion, and a gentle compression or softening of the chest initiates both ground force reaction and the forward drive from the top.

TRY THIS NO. 13
THROWING A PUNCH

The punch is a basic movement in all the martial arts. We're going to use a version that's sometimes called beng chuan or crushing fist and which has a spiralling motion.

To begin, hold your right hand at the side of your waist, with your fist closed softly, fingers facing upwards and thumb facing out away from the body. As you make the punch, your fist will come to the centre line of the body (nose to navel), finishing in front of the solar plexus, fingers facing inward, and your thumb on top. Your fist is relaxed but will close tightly at the moment of impact. You can create more momentum by beginning with your opposite fist in front of you and pulling it back when you punch as if you were pulling your opponent towards you by their belt.

You can also use the following to help.

i.   Wing Chun paper punching drill: put a pinprick in a sheet of A4 paper and thread through some cotton or string so you can hang it up in a door frame or suspend it from a wooden beam. The paper gives you a point of focus for your practice and helps you learn how to hit through the target.

ii. Boxing focus pads; be careful with this drill: wear hand wraps or gloves and build up your precision before adding power. You'll need the help of a friend to hold the focus pads for you and ask them to provide a little resistance for you to strike.

Try a few air punches to get going. Stand in a shoulder-width 'horse stance', one foot in front of the other. Your weight is on the back leg. Notice how the intent-driven punch is a pure movement that's so applicable to golf. Your body will respond instinctively to the simple intention in your mind; you will naturally bend your knees to lower your centre of gravity, turn your waist, shift the weight forward and extend your punching arm; you don't have to think about it as your *bodymind* is automatically responding to the idea.

Now you're going to try the paper punching drill. You're going for a lightness of touch, precision and extending through the target. Punch alternately with your left and right fist.

Notice how the punch is initiated by the condition of relaxed readiness as the body prepares itself for the movement.

As the idea becomes stronger, you'll feel a slight compression into the ground that transfers energy up through the waist and into the fist.

Next, you'll try punching a focus pad, or you can stay with the paper punching but have the intention that instead of a light tap, you're going to deliver a heavy blow. You could even make yourself a traditional wall bag using an old pillowcase filled with some dry rice or beans. Be advised: it's quite tough on the hands as there is no spring back from the wall!

As you prepare to deliver a more devastating blow, you'll feel how the set-up for the punch is from the inside first, as you crunch down or compress into the ground before using the upwards pressure thus generated to strike. Your body will respond automatically to the various different forces by bending the knees, tightening the core, lowering the centre of gravity and adjusting the speed of delivery.

A punch contains all the same set-up and movement requirements as a golf shot yet will deliver the intended outcome without any thought about individual positions because the intention is clear and the sequence happens naturally; we just do it.

The punch does not decelerate as a highly choreographed swing tends to do, as the impetus or focus of intent is to hit *through* the target.

When we set-up for the punch, we intuitively respond to the circumstances, be they a modest tap or something more aggressive, and the ensuing set-up can range from being close to a normal stance for the light tap to a very solid, almost unmoveable base for that more aggressive delivery. It is the same for golf.

You can go through the theoretical steps to produce what may look like an orthodox set-up over the ball, but the mind and body will only work together to execute the shot if the whole process is born of a clear inner intention. As such, the set-up is from the 'inside' rather than the 'outside'.

These intentional movements are easy to understand, and the body can respond almost effortlessly to the idea. Applying this to golf, it becomes apparent that when we call the golfing movement a 'swing', these fundamental laws of movement are not adhered to, which is possibly one of the reasons why conventional coaching resorts to teaching a sequence of various positions.

A more instinctive, natural and reproducible movement is similar to the ball slam exercise or straight punch and can develop into a 'splitting fist' type of punch from Hsing-Yi that is said to rise and fall like an axe. We saw earlier that one of the world's elite coaches likens the motion of the swing to striking a nail with a hammer. As such, approaching the golf swing like a strike gives a different impetus to the entire movement, especially at the top of the backswing, in order to make the transition.

We'll look at this more closely in Chapter Eleven: Delivering Your Intent, to help you shift from thinking about technique to focusing on delivering your intention so your body can respond naturally and instinctively as it has done with the two exercises you've just tried.

First, you're going to build a more connected set-up.

CHAPTER TEN

THE CONNECTED SET-UP

"This firm stance, free of all tension, must lead the archer to feel that he embodies a link between heaven and earth."

Hans Joachim Stein

The connected set-up is a way of summoning TMB before taking your shot. If your mind and body can be more related in the moments before you start moving, then movement itself will be more connected. All the learning, 'TRY THIS' suggestions and other exercises in this book are to help you get out of your head and into the body when you're standing over the ball.

You don't need to throw all swing thoughts aside but develop a regular practice or discipline so that you can stay connected to your feet, your centre, your breathing and a simple awareness of being on the golf course. This might sound easy enough, but the more you think through the mechanics of your shot, the harder you try to get it right, the more you focus on that little white ball, the more you disappear into the analytical mind and its mistaken assumption that it can play the shot for you.

The origins of this approach to a more conscious life go back many thousands of years; in Sanskrit, the term *abhyasa* is used to denote the constant repetitive effort of focusing on simple things like the posture and the breathing. From the Yoga Sutras of Patanjali, we learn to 'maintain steadiness and ease' in meditation. From the Chinese martial arts, we are taught whole-body awareness and integrated movement, while other teachers, such as the inimitable G.I. Gurdjieff, pointed the way towards 'a collected state' which arises from an intentional effort to stay close to the sensation of the physical body and its energy.

It's a very deep subject, and you are encouraged to explore it further using the bibliography and resources in the back of this book. For our purposes, we are taking our cues from the martial and Zen arts of China and Japan, which give detailed and precise instructions for using the simplest training repeated time and time over, and its applications when preparing for movement.

In Japanese archery, for instance, we have already seen the term *yugamae*, which means 'being prepared' with regards to both inner concentration and the external technical aspects of releasing the arrow towards the target.

Mind, body and technique form a harmonious whole, fully integrated and concentrated within the lower body, particularly the hara (t'an tien) and the lower legs and feet. In this way, the upper and lower parts of the body do not become two separate halves but remain a unity until the release has been completed. From this level of inner concentration, intuitive correction of minor faults in bodily posture and technique becomes possible, without resorting to a mental checklist.

Certainly, the feedback from my students, both men and women, who have committed themselves to this training, report an increased intuition whether reflecting on instructions from their swing professional, adjusting their posture on the range or trusting their abilities on the course.

In the Chinese martial arts from the Wu Tang or *internal* schools, teachings exist on what are called the external and internal 'harmonies', which help mind, body and spirit align for a single purpose.

We'll look at these briefly before giving guidelines on how you can apply them to golf; we'll take the ideas and apply them to your set-up, going deeper than before into these moments of preparation for the shot.

A wonderful phrase used by one of my students to relay his experience is that 'setting up from the inside allows me to intuitively deliver my intent'.

EXTERNAL HARMONIES

The shoulders match the hips, the elbows match the knees and the hands match the feet.

In today's terminology from sports science and biomechanics, we might express these harmonies as joint-stacking, whereby the upper body is contained within the framework of the lower body; as such, it can respond to the impulses or instructions it receives from the legs and waist. I don't believe this is the case with the orthodox set-up, and I will explain why with some suggestions on improving it shortly.

What's useful here is that paying attention to such fundamentals like emptying the chest, being physically centred and balanced and loading the psoas (creasing the 'kwa') helps prepare the body to move in the most efficient way *without* having to run through a menu of swing positions in your mind.

If it's helpful, you can think of the external harmonies like a straight line from your shoulder, down through your hip, to the knee and foot. Adhering to these during your swing can stop the tendency to fall back at impact with the reverse 'c' shape, which is a common fault many players experience.

INTERNAL HARMONIES

The heart matches the mind, the mind matches the chi and the chi matches the strength.

We haven't delved into the vast subject of 'chi', even though the internal arts we've been studying seek to strengthen and utilise this vital energy for combative, healing and spiritual purposes. The reason is that this whole work is enough of a paradigm shift in itself.

Moreover, the training is not just about applying one movement art (Tai Chi) to another (golf) to become 'Tai Chi golf' but is a synergy which creates something entirely new. This something is a **Performance Practice** which can be applied to *any* situation where complex movement has to be released under pressure, whether that's golf, tennis, swimming, figure skating or in the performance arts like music and dance.

Looking very simply at the internal harmonies, we see that they've been touched upon earlier when we looked at the Tai Chi concept of movement arising first from an idea or intention, secondly from the energy in the body and lastly from the physical action.

The subtle or energy body, which can be developed with various training methods, gives the physical body its life and movement. You may start to notice this when doing the paper punching drill, staying loose and relaxed and closing your fist at the last minute. You can also develop this awareness when performing a 'shock punch' against the wall bag or focus pad. The shock is generated by a recoiling motion of the waist at the same moment the punch connects with the bag. Feel how the energy within your body responds to your intention: in other words, how your chi (energy) responds to the Yi (intent). It happens much quicker than your analytical mind can keep up with!

Chi, in essence, is connection, the delivery of energy in the most direct route through the joints or 'gates' of the body. In golf, when you make the swing an integrated whole-body movement, where the relaxed upper body responds to the shifting weight of the lower body and the rotation through the t'an tien, you will generate more stored energy, increasing your clubhead speed and power.

As one of my students, Matt C., a PGA coach, remarked, "I have never liked the way my upper body and lower body have looked at the top. Not very dynamic! I don't think I have ever truly understood how I can achieve more separation. This is definitely the key to increasing the power through impact."

Before we look at a new way of setting up over the ball, let's review the concept of 'sung' and the four fundamental actions and see how they correspond to the external and internal harmonies.

The most essential quality you can have before taking your shot is a feeling of relaxed readiness. Your body should feel athletic but not taut or tight in any way. Your mind will echo this state by being gently focused within, and a quiet concentration on the t'an tien will help slow down and deepen your breathing, getting you close to the meditative or flow-state.

Standing over the ball, you can prepare your physical body for connected movement by applying the four fundamentals, which are (i) empty the chest, (ii) gently pull in the centre, (iii) load the muscles at the tops of the legs and (iv) find the balance point on the feet. These actions are sequential and related to each other. Although you might have to separate them out to start with, i.e. do them individually, after training the Standing Meditation for a short while, it will become more natural, and the four actions can be applied in the time it takes to exhale one breath.

As previously mentioned, we're looking to replicate the internal conditions experienced during your practice swings or before the effortless strike of the ball and drill these conditions so they can be in place when you're standing over those pressure shots.

When these conditions exist, i.e. when your mind is quiet yet gently focused, your breathing is slow and relaxed, your body is primed without being tense, and the strength is in the legs, you'll gain a sense of clarity about your intended outcome, and your body will be able to move freely.

As Tai Chi Grandmaster Cai Song Fang explains, "The quality of our contact with the earth through our feet affects in a deep way the growth and expansion of our awareness, mind and spirit."

A connected golfer plays connected golf; setting up from the inside, you align your attention within your physical body, gaining a closer relationship between your mental state and your intention for physical action. This external and internal alignment helps to summon TMB, which, in turn, allows complex movement to be released with ease.

TRY THIS NO. 14
THE CONNECTED SET-UP

The most important thing about the connected set-up is the fact that your lower body provides the support and stability for your upper body, which in turn, must be loose and relaxed. Moreover, the upper body must be placed in such a way that it can 'receive instruction' from the lower body in order to move, instructions that arise primarily from the weight distribution in the feet and the turning of the waist. Your arms must feel and respond to the impetus for both horizontal and vertical movement, which arise in the lower body.

To achieve this, we must make an important distinction between this new way of addressing the ball and the orthodox set-up. Many of my students, from competitive amateurs to golf coaches and professional tour players, have worked with this approach, and given their consent that the methods of **Connected Golf** work at all levels of the game and are a preferable alternative to the mainstream industry approach..

In the mainstream world of golf, players often set-up on the balls of the feet and from this position hinge forward from the hips, which means their upper body hangs out in space with little stability or true connection to the legs or the ground. It also puts additional strain on the knees rather than letting the muscles at the tops of the legs support the body.

When you begin from such an unbalanced and top-heavy posture, the arms tend to lead the motion as, together with the torso, they have become independent and therefore disconnected from the kinetic chain.

I often advise my students to watch Bruce Lee movies as part of their training and to try and set-up *Bruce Lee-style* over the ball. This entails softening, loosening and emptying the upper body so that it is fully supported by the 'kwa' or psoas muscles and the feet. If you doubt the additional power and accuracy this can generate in your golf swing, remember that at just over 5ft 7inches (1.72 m) and with a body-fat index of less than 8%, Lee could knock a man flying with a punch generated from just one inch away from his opponent's body. Now that's ground force energy!

Lee would always crunch down or compress into the ground before throwing a punch or kick, and if you drill the following steps at set-up, you'll have the sort of relaxed yet athletic swing that will help you maximise your potential.

1. First, you're going to hold the club in the air parallel to the ground so that you can check your grip and alignment.

2. Then you'll set the clubhead down, aim it towards the target, step in and align your feet.

3. As you do this, exhale slowly while you simultaneously apply the four fundamental actions.

4. Now you're the right distance from the ball, in a perfectly balanced, strong but relaxed posture from which to slowly take away the club.

5. To incorporate your breathing, maintain a point of focus on the t'an tien and inhale to the top of your backswing. Then at the top, you will begin your exhale as you re-apply the four fundamental actions and continue to exhale through impact.

6. Practise slowly after doing the Standing Meditation, and you'll see how easy and natural it is to apply this inner movement from chest to feet as you breathe out.

Remember, this is *not* a mental checklist. You are preparing the body using simple and subtle physical actions that are proven to harmonise idea and action and to summon integrated movement by connecting to the higher intelligence of the *bodymind*.

Try to *feel* what's happening rather than thinking your way through it. As you train the Standing Meditation and other drills (see Part Three) and develop your ability to move from your centre, these internal actions will happen automatically, so that idea, energy and motion are all united.

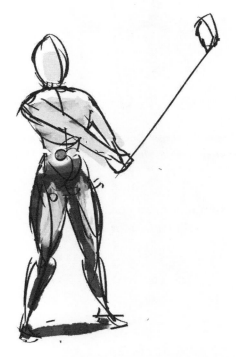

Figure 9: Checking Your Grip and Alignment

Figure 10: Empty the Upper Body – as you set the clubhead down, relax your shoulders, empty your chest and load the legs

Now you've set-up in a more connected way, let's see how it can help you deliver your intention for the shot.

CHAPTER ELEVEN

DELIVERING YOUR INTENT

"From posture to posture, the internal power is unbroken."

Tai Chi Classics

Connected Golf offers a thread of constancy that can run through all aspects of your game, whether that's practising on the range, honing instructions from your swing coach, experiencing more enjoyment on the course or performing at the highest level under pressure. This thread comes from the two pillars of correct breathing and the application of fundamental movement skills, both of which are integral to the release of complex movement in a way that is effortless when it matters most.

In Chapter Five: Three Levels of Performance, we saw that this approach actually leads the way to the highest expression of the game, level three on the Performance Pyramid. This level, which usually appears by accident, can, in fact, be trained, provided we clearly understand and accept the truth about how the perfect golf shot arose in the first place.

As such, we are changing our emphasis, perspective and training to focus on developing and maintaining a state of relaxed readiness (sung) in which we are replicating the internal conditions necessary for the flow-state to appear and which enables the release of natural movement by connecting mind to body, idea to action.

I truly hope you have understood how important it is not to rush off to the practice range and try things from this book without applying yourself to the training; these aren't tips and tricks or ideas I've come up with, but centuries-old principles and practices to develop the *bodymind*. What you're reading took decades of work, extracting the essential elements from the martial and Zen arts and applying them to golf and sports performance.

This training is to awaken a particular state or quality and to maintain this in both preparation and in movement. Remember the order of training in the martial arts: first, the practitioner trains in stillness, holding certain postures for extended periods of time, then they take this enhanced awareness into slow motion and empty-hand movements before finally taking up a weapon such as a sword.

In this way, the inner connections developed in stillness can be applied in movement. There is no room for analytical thoughts about how to move the sword, just an instantaneous reaction to the situation.

Here's a passage from *The Mysterious Record of Immovable Wisdom* by Zen master Takuan Soho (1573-1645) in conversation with the famous swordsman Yagyu Munenori.

> *"To speak in terms of your own martial art, when you first notice the sword that is moving to strike you, if you think of meeting that sword just as it is, your mind will stop at the sword in just that position, your own movements will be undone, and you will be cut down by your opponent… If ten men, each with a sword, come at you with swords slashing, if you parry each sword without stopping the mind at each action, and you go from one to the next, you will not be lacking in a proper action for every one of the ten. Although the mind acts ten times against ten men, if it does not halt at even one of them and you react to one after another, will proper action be lacking? But if the mind stops before one of these men, though you parry his striking sword, when the next man comes, the right action will have slipped away."*

In the same way, your golf shot can become a pure reaction to what's needed in that particular moment if you can shift your emphasis away from analytical thinking and towards a more mindful way of preparing yourself to strike the ball. The analogy used previously was the necessity to train the operator (golfer) as well as the golfing machine.

This is why abhyasa or constant repetitive effort is so important; the path from intent through energy and into action can be so easily interfered with and interrupted by the mind.

The Standing Meditation and other drills are to help your body respond naturally, instinctively and spontaneously to the intention.

Moreover, they will help you to keep your connected set-up in place while moving through the motion of your swing.

By drilling down into the very structure of the body, we can see how it can best be developed for supporting, enhancing and releasing your swing using a wisdom and insight that has reached us through generations of the same lineage, often of the same family, practising a particular art.

I was in the clubhouse recently talking with one of the PGA coaches I work with when a pupil of his walked by the table. They spoke for a few moments, and Andy (the pro) advised his student to improve his set-up by 'sinking into the ground and relaxing the upper body'. This, of course, is true. Yet the ensuing conversation that Andy and I had following his casual remark was that this training clearly pinpoints the specific locations in the body that can turn the instruction he gave from a great idea into a workable methodology.

The structure of the lower body, when properly balanced, coupled with a relaxed upper body, when correctly softened, enables free rotation through the waist, the delivery of connected movement and better contact with the ball.

These principles, which have all been thoroughly documented in the previous chapters, can serve to replace many unnecessary swing thoughts. This is important not only at set-up but when moving through the 1.8 seconds of the golf swing where so often the attention flits from one swing thought to another.

We've already looked at how to go from stillness to movement, and when in movement, it's vital that you don't abandon the principles which enabled you to set-up with a more relaxed yet athletic quality. This will become particularly important when you're under pressure.

When you are connected at set-up, your upper body will react according to the impulses coming from your lower body and your intention. The t'an tien, often referred to as a 'second brain' in the Eastern arts as it responds to and is a component of intent, shows this attribute has nothing to do with the analytical mind.

The feedback from my students demonstrates how feelings such as 'moving from the centre' had previously been experienced when they played their best golf. It echoes what was said about the preparation of the archer, and even though these things are not taught in the mainstream, golfers still touch upon these sensations in those accidental moments of flow. This is because they are part of the laws of human motion and appear when mind and body are more related, which can only happen when you get out of your own way.

What I've always found interesting about the response to my work is that hobbyists tend to argue against it, but the higher up in golf I have taught this methodology, especially in recent years to teaching and playing professionals, the more they concur that it absolutely makes sense.

The connected set-up can help you deliver the type of shot you want to play, which will include the ball position selected and the intended delivery of the clubhead if you can stay with an awareness of the fundamental actions of the lower body throughout the shot rather than getting lost in the minutiae of swing positions.

Again, the swing feelings or points of physical awareness that help to connect your swing are the balance points on the feet just below the tibia bone, the creasing of the "kwa" or loading of the psoas muscle at the tops of the legs and a free rotation through the t'an tien.

When we use this internal energy map or model of the human body as per the soft-style martial arts, swing feelings can be maintained throughout the shot, including that of a three-dimensional pivot-point or centre of rotation from which centrifugal force can be generated.

To deliver your intent, your idea and the ensuing physical actions must marry up, so in the next exercise, we're going to look at a golf *strike* as opposed to a golf *swing*, building on the idea posited by some of the top golf coaches that hitting a golf ball is fundamentally the same movement as driving a nail with a hammer.

Yet, as you'll see, when we employ martial arts wisdom to train this motion, it becomes a feeling in the body anchored within certain parameters rather than an idea about movement.

First, we need to look at another important concept from Tai Chi which will be extremely useful for delivering your intent to strike rather than swing at the ball; this concept is 'fa jin' which means 'to explode or issue power'.

From the martial arts, we learn that power is the result of structure plus relaxation; when standing in meditation, the skeleton and tendons hold the body in place, while the musculature in turn can relax. The lower body forms a strong connection with the ground, and the upper body resides within the framework of the lower body while maintaining a certain liveliness arising from the idea of the head being suspended from above. At the same time, the chest empties or hollows, softening the front of the body and lowering the centre of gravity.

These opposing forces or differing qualities in the spine and chest, and the lower and upper body, are what allow the arms and torso to spin around the centre without losing balance, speed or power.

Fa jin utilises these forces, maintaining both softness and strength in a slow and relaxed winding up before a devastating and explosive release. You've already practised this in your punching drills by staying as loose as possible until the very moment you close your fist and hit through the target.

The inner connections are made first: a deep relaxation and a sinking of the mind, the chest, the shoulders, the breathing and the intention for movement towards the t'an tien, which can then freely rotate away from a stable lower body, including the hips, thus building up energy.

The result is a spontaneous moment of perfection when everything comes together, whether it's drawing a sword from its sheath, painting an ensō circle with a single stroke of a calligraphy brush or releasing an arrow from the bow. The unification of the *bodymind*, usually fragmented and separated in everyday life, is brought together through a particular effort, which then allows even the most complex movement to be effortlessly released.

This is not philosophy but a way to train the inner conditions that allow the perfect movement to manifest itself in a single moment; it cannot be forced, it is not dependent on willpower, athleticism, knowledge of technique or anything to do with the psychology of the practitioner, but comes from a realm higher than the everyday mind can comprehend. To wit: it cannot even keep up with the speed at which intent, energy and action can be released.

When your body is primed 'like a perfectly tensioned bow', you can use fa jin to turn your golf swing into a pure strike of the ball.

TRY THIS NO. 15
THE GOLF STRIKE

The strike will vary according to your intention, including the type of shot and ball position selected and whether you intend to hit downwards on the ball for your iron shots or up and out for your driver. These decisions require you to intuitively decide on the impact position so that your set-up and ensuing movement are all adjusted to deliver the outcome.

There are many, many theories and therefore discrepancies within the mainstream about all these technicalities, including various instructions about where the hands are in relation to the ball. To conform to Tai Chi principles, you might like to try starting with the hands a little forward so you can 'borrow' the momentum from your legs and waist to turn in the opposite direction first.

You may have a picture in mind about the shot you want to play that you then set-up to, and some of my students who've been working with this methodology for some time can feel how the body and also the grip responds to their intention such that their set-up posture gives instruction to the body about the required impact position.

It's useful to take a couple of practice swings and, as previously mentioned, to try and maintain your internal state as you set-up to the ball for real.

From your connected set-up, you will not deviate from the balance points on the feet or the muscles at the tops of the legs but let them support your upper body, which you will keep relaxed to aid the free rotation of the waist. You can still shift your weight from one foot to the other, but the tendency to move laterally will be eliminated.

At the top, provided you have maintained the strength in your legs and distinguished your hips from your waist, you will feel a separation that is difficult to hold as your body will be primed like a rubber band stretched in two directions. This is the essence of fa jin as you've stored the energy to strike using the entire structure or frame of the body, rather than isolated or individual parts.

Now you'll reinforce the internal compression of the body to begin your transition.

Nicklaus said that "the downswing is the application of power and accuracy through the release of the golf club from the feet up"; applying the four fundamentals of emptying the chest, engaging the centre, loading the legs and reinforcing the balance point will help you feel this in your own game. With practice, it will only take a moment and can be initiated by the start of your exhalation, which will continue through impact and to your finish position.

Figure 11: Reconnect in Transition — activate the lower body by reapplying the four fundamentals to begin your downswing

Again, you will adhere to the balance points in the feet and the tops of the legs while you move through impact, where you will accelerate and transfer the energy through the ball with the same intent you used in the punch exercise. Your finish position should be as balanced and stable as your set-up.

You can develop this exercise in the following ways:

i.   Practise it in slow motion, which will really help you *feel* how all movement is initiated from the ground upwards. Your tempo will be 3-1, meaning it will take three times as long to move from set-up to the top than to strike down and through impact. Notice how you can stay relatively relaxed during the initial stage of the movement when you are winding up the power and how the intent to strike rather than swing encourages a change in how your body moves from the top and through the transition. The movement may feel more whip-like and will stop you trying to muscle through the ball.

ii.   Going slowly, you will also notice any tightness and tension in the body and how much your mind wants to interfere and take over. Use the slow motion practice to train your attention to reside in the centre of gravity for the duration of the shot; this will help you relax your chest and shoulders and use your lower body more efficiently.

iii. Once you are comfortable practising the strike slowly, you can try to incorporate your breathing in the same way martial arts practitioners use their out-breath to deliver more power through the target. For this, point (ii) above is vitally important; if you can keep your awareness in your physical centre, your breathing will stay deep and slow down, eliminating many feelings of anxiety.

iv.   Breathe out as you hit through the ball using the same 'kiai' sound that occurs when the energy is released during a punch or kick. To employ this 'spirit shout' appropriately, it must come from the hara/t'an tien and not the chest or throat as some female tennis players are prone to do. Used mostly in Japanese martial arts like Karate, the kiai is represented by the ideograms for 'energy' and 'join', respectively. The sound is both a compressing and delivering of stored energy in an instant release. Practise this on the range rather than on the course. During play, you can eliminate the sound but still exhale while pushing your diaphragm down to the hara.

In one of my favourite martial arts, called Hsing-Yi, literally 'the mind forms the fist', the type of punch (splitting, crushing, drilling, upper-cut and crossing) responds to the practitioner's intention, which in turn arises due to the situation and the opponent. The moment of impact or delivery of the fist to the target begins with an idea and ends in the appropriate action.

In golf, many elite players like Dame Laura Davies, England's most accomplished female golfer, concur that the movement from the top down is the most crucial part of hitting the ball in the correct way for the type of shot to be played.

As a strike, the movement from the top becomes more natural and instinctive, and whether hitting down or upwards onto the ball, the ensuing motion can form around your intention without having to think your way through a number of static positions. It just happens in the same way that the perfect shot usually occurs by accident, although now you know how to recreate it.

The laws of human motion, including the kinetic chain, escalation, vertical force and so on, are all adhered to and occur naturally without you having to force anything so long as you have the parameters or pillars in place; then the complexities of the movement can happen without the necessity to think about it or interfere because you are adhering to certain principles that remain true all the time, even under pressure.

The training will help in ways you can't even comprehend for now, including strengthening your attention so that you can divide it between picturing the shot you want to make and staying with the physical sensation of your breathing or your feet on the ground.

Your Standing Meditation and the other drills and exercises will help you stay focused on your intention for the shot instead of changing your mind halfway through the movement or having a different swing thought every time you set-up.

Let's complete your intention training with the following exercise, going deeper into the subject than that used in the mental game approach.

TRY THIS NO. 16
SEEING THE SHOT

"I never hit a shot, not even in practice, without having a very sharp, in-focus picture of it in my head. It's like a color movie. First, I 'see' where I want it to finish, nice and white and sitting up high on the bright green grass. Then the scene quickly changes and I 'see' the ball going there: its path, trajectory and shape, even its behaviour on landing. Then there is this sort of fadeout, and the next scene shows me making the kind of swing that will turn the previous images to reality." **Jack Nicklaus**

What's so interesting about the approach used by Nicklaus is that neuroscientists have only recently proven that visualising the process is as important as visualising the desired outcome.

Visualisation or visual motor rehearsal is more powerful when you have a clear picture in your mind of the type of swing you need to make to produce the shot you want, as well as seeing the flight of the ball and where you want it to finish.

All of the training in this book is to help you develop a keener awareness of your body, your mind, your emotional state and your breathing as you prepare to take the club away, and how this either interferes with, or lays the groundwork for, the release of natural movement.

The standing posture and slow motion exercises, in particular, will help you strengthen your proprioception, which is your internal map of where your body is in space and time. In the conventional approach, which encourages both technical and mental game thoughts when you're standing over the ball, the tendency is to move towards CFM and away from TMB.

Remember the Tai Chi adage that 'stillness is the master of motion' and be consistent with your training to develop a greater feel for your own physicality and how your body wants to move without trying to force or control it. You will then be able to go through the appropriate actions to deliver the swing necessary to play your best shot.

This will be greatly enhanced if, during your visualisation sequence, you are able to maintain a simple awareness of your breathing and any physical sensation like your grip or your feet on the ground so that you stay 'present' and don't disappear into the mind.

Otherwise, visualisation will become just another layer of things to think about rather than a key part of your intention for the shot.

Let's finish your introduction to this new paradigm in golf performance by showing how the principles and practices of **Connected Golf** can help you play your best game, even under the most intense pressure.

CHAPTER TWELVE

PERFORMING UNDER PRESSURE

"Do your best and leave the rest to heaven."

Japanese proverb

What does it mean to perform under pressure? Does it mean a winning mindset, being mentally tough, and crushing your opponents, or does it mean being able to produce the shot you want when you're in contention as if you were on the driving range and nobody was watching?

One thing that's always struck me about books that have been written to help athletes perform under pressure is that, very often, they give a general summation of psychological techniques that could just as easily be applied in business or education. This teaching is different as we've looked at the very thing golfers and athletes from all sports need to perform in the white heat of competition, and that is complex movement. It's very different from what's required of a chief executive or an undergraduate.

Performing under pressure actually means delivering the subtle complexity of a great golf swing in a way that is fluid, powerful and effortless when you absolutely have to make the shot. This is why your training is so important. As a new student, Ryan W. from Wisconsin recently remarked after playing a less stressful and more enjoyable round, consistently envisioning and producing his desired outcome, "Trusting there is a higher intelligence and giving it an intention means holding an empty mind and losing the ego."

Well said.

As we've seen, it's the quality of the golfer's *inner connections* that lead to connected movement; this is brought about by making a consistent effort to bring the attention to the breathing, the t'an tien, and the feet, relaxing the upper body and applying the four fundamentals over the ball. When these foundations are in place, they will ensure your natural swing is locked down because you have adhered to the principles of movement, which begin with a state of relaxed readiness in the moments before you start moving.

The beauty of the methodology you've been learning is that it applies in all situations, whether you are practising, honing your skills, playing or indeed performing at the highest level or under any circumstances when you're in contention and the stakes are high.

In the Introduction, I mentioned how difficult it was for so many years to understand what my role was in golf, as I am neither a swing coach nor a mental game coach, and I don't play the game. I hope you can see now that it's only because of these things that this new paradigm has been developed or, rather, uncovered, as it was there all along in the Eastern arts.

Every revolution is a revolution of ideas and the biggest idea for you to take from this work is that you, the golfer, are not responsible for hitting the perfect shot. Nor is it your responsibility to try and make the perfect swing. Instead, the onus of your attention needs to be on replicating the internal conditions (TMB) that allows for the spontaneous arising of complex movement in the most sublime and effortless way. As mentioned before, this is not simply philosophy, but a teaching that has been passed down through successive generations of martial and Zen practitioners, which we have examined together and applied to golf.

As one of my PGA students remarked, your training is 'payment' for playing connected golf. If you wish to continue this path, all your efforts now will be on making those vital connections, i.e. connecting mind to body, connecting upper body to lower body and connecting to the ground.

As we saw in Chapter Five: Three Levels of Performance, the requirement for playing the highest expression of the game corresponds perfectly to the third Performance Paradox, which states, 'To obtain the desired outcome, focus on the process'.

The process referred to is using exactly the same meditative postures and drills in your deep practice training when preparing for a tournament, walking out to the first tee and standing over those pressure shots.

Often, the results are immediate and astounding, to wit: the countless messages I've received from golfers all over the world who have dropped shots off their handicaps, played the round of their life or won a club competition or professional tournament for the first time ever. People often remark, 'I couldn't believe that was really me playing', or express gratitude for being able to get out of their own way and finally enjoy being in the game.

I gently remind them that the real work has only just begun; as the proverb goes, 'After the victory, tighten the cords of your helmet'. In other words, keep training.

Early on in this new journey, it will be tempting to abandon the principles when things start to unravel, and the tightness, tension and mental interference you might be so familiar with once again come to the fore.

When this happens, you will no doubt engage in self-talk to the effect that I'm not a golf coach, so I don't know what I'm talking about, what I'm teaching is too simple to be really effective and focusing on your feet can't possibly help you stay in the shot. It's also likely you'll start talking to yourself about your performance, your technique and even revert to swing thoughts, tinkering with your grip and the mechanics of individual positions, trying to muscle your way through the ball.

Please try to remember that what's being asked of you is very real work, of a different calibre to psychological or technical thinking and harder even than training your body in the gym. You are embarking on a remarkable journey of self-exploration, the ultimate prize for which is the ability to have mastery over yourself and your game.

This book took over a decade to research, develop with my students and write, and the methodology itself is the result of over thirty years' personal training and exploration of the relationship between inner stillness and effortless motion. What you're learning is, I believe, an essential Performance Practice, which is now taking hold with golfers and athletes of many different sports in over 20 countries around the world.

That's what's on offer here for you.

In this so-called information age of instant fixes, where everybody has an opinion or can set themselves up as an online expert, what you're being encouraged to do, i.e. make consistent, repetitive effort over many weeks, months and years, is counter to everything life is throwing at you.

Here are three simple things you can do to sustain your belief in all that this book is offering so that you can trust the teachings and apply them when the pressure's on.

DO THE TRAINING

Try to practise for at least 15–20 minutes each day; begin with Standing Meditation. If you're incorporating the learning from **Breathe Golf,** you might like to sit for 15 minutes before standing or even alternate your seated and standing practice on different days.

Following this, warm up your body to deliver the kinetic chain (feet, waist and hands) by doing the 'Moving the Centre' drills from Part Three before some slow motion golf swings. It's also useful to do these on the range before heading out to the course. You can then do some of the TRY THIS exercises and golf-specific drills and make sure you write up your insights and reflections.

Keep everything the same when you're preparing for a tournament. It's usual for nerves and anxiety to begin around three weeks before the actual event, causing you to imagine all kinds of negative scenarios and making it difficult to sleep, so the more consistent you are with your practice, the better.

As the day of the competition draws near, try doing short bursts of meditation, sitting or standing quietly and taking a few breaths with your attention firmly on your t'an tien; this 'inward look', as my student Norm B. from British Columbia calls it, will help you feel more centred and balanced and put a stop to any mental-interference.

On the course, you can come back to this any time you start to feel anxious or overexcited. Standing a little apart from your competitors with your hands gently cupping the navel area, you can be going through the four fundamental actions or simply feeling your feet on the ground while waiting for your turn to play.

LISTEN TO YOUR BODY

On the course, look for signs and symptoms that you're coming away from flow or going down the imaginary snakes and ladders board towards Level Two: Good Days, Bad Days or worse, Level One: Search for a Swing.

Your body is always giving you clues and signals which equate to not feeling comfortable over the ball, and, with your training, you will develop a keen awareness so you can identify exactly what's happening and take the necessary steps to regroup. For instance, the most common symptom of pressure is rushing, not only your preparation but the swing itself; making the effort to slow down can be helped enormously by getting in touch with the sensation of the physical body. Other ways pressure shows up are gripping the club too tightly, holding your breath and not feeling balanced.

These are all warning signs telling you to hold back, step away and take a moment before setting up again.

It might seem an easy fix, but we've seen countless elite players make this crucial mistake of playing a shot before really settling over the ball. Without a Performance Practice, it's difficult to see yourself doing this and harder still to interrupt the chain reaction caused by stress. The intention to switch the biochemistry back to neutral or into the relaxation response requires tremendous effort and cannot be accomplished using psychological interventions.

You always have more time than you think and can easily wait a few moments to get into the body without holding up play. In particular, your connection to the ground is vitally important for steadying the nerves and stopping negative thought-chains and holding to your centre will help you feel calmer and quietly confident.

As Nicklaus and others have said, the only adversaries you have in golf are yourself and the golf course so pay attention to everything your body is trying to tell you, and then prime it in the correct way so it can respond to your intention.

When you're on the course, be there! Listen to the birdsong, hear the breeze rustling through the leaves and see the shadows of the setting sun on the fairway. Opening the peripheral vision by looking to the horizon (as you'll do in your Standing Meditation) activates the occipital lobe and helps get you in flow.

You'll find so many benefits and myriad ways this approach can help raise your game and your enjoyment level that it will be hard to think that these ancient practices weren't deliberately made for golf in the first place! Standing on the tee, you'll be able to see the shot you want to play while simultaneously staying within your own body, calmly yet purposefully preparing to hit the ball. Getting out of your own way, you will have prepared for intention and action to align, allowing your body to do what it knows how to do without the usual self-interference.

GIVE IT TIME

As mentioned in **Breathe Golf**, you have to make time for flow to manifest when you're standing over the ball. Neuroscientists have estimated that we can hold our attention for roughly 12 seconds, which doesn't say much for humanity, unfortunately, but it is good news for golfers. With consistent training and those short bursts of breathing and body awareness you'll be practising leading up to the day of competition, you will only need a few seconds of inner quiet to become firmly established within yourself before taking the shot.

Golfers have long complained that there's too much time to think, but that isn't really the point. It's true that in these moments, the default tendency is to go through a mental checklist, and this, of course, has been encouraged by the fading paradigm of the orthodox approach, which will have you think about how you're going to move and think about how you're thinking. As you know by now, all this accomplishes is the further activation of CFM and the fragmentation of movement.

With your training, you can instead choose to use the time to encourage mind and body to unite, which, in turn, invites the flow-state to appear and enhances the quality of your movement. See the shot; let your body respond and commit.

Above all, seek connection, and everything else will follow.

"I have to feel the body on the earth, the ground. I do this by sensation, sensing its weight, its mass, and, more important, sensing that there is a force inside, an energy... When I obey the earth's attraction in a conscious way, the subtle force is liberated, and my... ego finds its place, its purpose. But thinking it does not help. I must live it."

Jeanne de Salzmann

PART THREE

CHAPTER THIRTEEN

TRAINING AND DRILLS

"I do not fear the warrior with a thousand techniques, but the warrior who has practised one technique a thousand times."

Wong Jack Man

SEATED MEDITATION

The bedrock of this entire approach, seated meditation (commonly known as Zazen), which uses the breathing as a point of focus, is proven to quieten the mind, reduce anxiety and allows for freedom of movement. It is the cornerstone of all the martial and Zen arts of the Eastern world.

You are invited to read (or re-read) my previous book *Breathe Golf* for key points on this formal and traditional practice and its applications to your game. Practising alongside the training given in *Connected Golf*, you will have approximately 80% of the learning shared with my personal students.

As previously stated, some of the subtleties of this inner work and movement exercises that incorporate softening and stretching of the body's connective tissue are beyond the scope of this book.

STANDING PRACTICE

This is the foundational practice for developing your mind-body connection, whole-body power, leg strength, ground force energy and the kinetic chain. It remains the essential training for the warrior monks of the Wudang and Shaolin traditions, and all modern-day practitioners of the martial arts train some form of Standing Meditation.

You are encouraged to train the following three postures, holding each posture, in order, for between three and ten minutes before moving on to the next.

Figure 12: Standing Posture No. 1 — Wu chi

Figure 13: Standing Posture No. 2 — Holding the ball

Figure 14: Standing Posture No. 3 – Holding the t'an tien

HOW TO PRACTISE

1. Stand with your feet shoulder-width apart and your toes pointing slightly outwards. Keep your knees in line with your toes by gently turning them out. Above all, don't let the knees collapse inwards.

2. Soften your knees without bending them too much to begin with and find the balance point, which is towards the front part of your heels, just behind the instep.

3. Gently tuck the coccyx under and slightly forwards to reduce the lumbar curve; your crown and tailbone ideally want to align, so keep your back straight and your head up, imagining it is suspended from above.

4. Relax your shoulders and soften your chest as if your sternum is sinking downwards.

5. Hold your hands at hip level to begin the exercise (*Wu chi*), imagining you are holding onto a large ball. If it's helpful, you can imagine sitting on a large ball too.

6. After a short while, bend your knees more while you simultaneously raise your hands to shoulder height (*Holding the ball*), taking care to relax your upper body, and let your legs support you. Even though your hands are raised, try not to lift the trapezium muscles. Let your elbows sink below the height of your hands.

7. Keep your chin tucked under to straighten the back of the head and look as far in front of you as possible, ideally at a pleasant scene of the natural world. If you are training indoors, imagine you can see through the wall into the distance.

8. Relax all your muscles, letting your bones and tendons hold the frame of the body.

9. Bring some attention to your breathing, letting the mind rest in the lower t'an tien, approximately two finger widths below the navel.

10. For the final posture, place your hands on the navel, one palm touching the body and the other palm touching the back of that hand.

TO FINISH

Bring your feet together. Raise your arms outwards to your sides and bring them up above your head while you breathe in; as you exhale, bring your palms down the centre line of the body to rest again at the t'an tien.

Do some slow walking for a few minutes (you'll find details in my eBook **The Practice of High-Performance**) and, if possible, go outside in nature. Try not to abandon your training for the rest of the day but come back into the body any time you remember.

DEVELOPING PENG

Standing in the second posture with your arms held at chest height as if you were holding a large ball, ask your golf partner to press down on your arms to see if they can disrupt your posture. Initially, you will try to use the muscles of the arms to ward them off, but if you keep practising, you will find that you can absorb or borrow their energy by compressing down into the ground, using the power of your legs to support the whole body.

In golf, this will translate into a greater awareness of your body, noticing tightness or tension and being able to relax while maintaining a strong yet pliable structure. You will also gain greater leg strength so the lower body can provide resistance against which your upper body will turn for your full swing. Many other benefits have already been explored, including the application of the four fundamental actions of standing practice at set-up.

MOVING THE CENTRE

These are traditional silk reeling exercises that train and develop the correct sequence of movement, as understood in Tai Chi. They are sometimes called 'opening the inner gates' and are referred to as 'rag doll' in my audio programme **Deep Practice for Effortless Golf** to illustrate how they loosen up the body.

The three exercises show the ideal way to warm up for your game, so do them on the practice range before heading out to the course.

They will help you develop three vital components of effortless or connected movement: (i) how to move from the bottom up, (ii) how to use the body's centre of gravity to generate centrifugal force and (iii) how to develop the correct order for natural movement, i.e. rooted in the feet, springing from the legs, guided by the waist and expressed in the hands.

Please be advised that these are movement exercises that can be useful to help develop the feeling of how the turning of the waist flings or propels the arms. You should aim to employ this learning in your golf for the movement from set-up to the top, allowing the lower body and the waist to naturally generate the motion of the arms. At the top, you will use the **Transition Drill** to reconnect with your lower body before once again allowing the upper body to respond to the impetus from your legs and waist.

Figure 15: Ready Posture

EXERCISE NO. 1
EMPTY YOUR CHEST AND TURN AROUND YOUR CENTRE

Stand with your feet shoulder-width apart and let your arms hang loosely by your sides. Make sure your posture corresponds to everything you have learned from the Standing Meditation, i.e. empty your chest, crease the 'kwa' and find the balance point.

Now simply turn from your waist, allowing the movement of the arms to be generated by the motion as if the waist is throwing the arms; this feeling will itself be initiated by a slight downward pressure into each of your feet in turn, i.e. when moving from the right side, you will feel the weight spring from your right foot, helping you turn to the left side and so forth.

Figure 16: Exercise No. 1 – Empty your chest and turn around your centre (right)

Figure 17: Exercise No. 1 – Empty your chest and turn around your centre (left)

EXERCISE NO. 2
EMPTY, TRANSFER YOUR WEIGHT AND TURN

Separate your feet more and begin the second exercise by deliberately transferring your weight from one foot to the other. You can keep your hands behind your back for a few moments while you get used to the feeling of transferring from left to right. Now let your arms hang freely while you continue to transfer your weight, letting the movement come from the legs and into the waist, propelling the arms as in the previous drill.

It's useful to try separating your hips from your waist while doing this exercise slowly. Allow your hips to turn no more than 45 degrees from the front before letting the waist take over and continue the rotation. If you do this correctly, you'll feel a 'lag' as the upper body *follows the instruction* given by the lower body and moves sequentially rather than at the same time.

**Figure 18: Exercise No. 2 –
Empty, transfer and turn (right)**

**Figure 19: Exercise No. 2 –
Empty, transfer and turn (left)**

EXERCISE NO. 3
EMPTY, TRANSFER AND TURN, LIFT THE HEEL

With your feet slightly wider (as above), you can now turn fully from one side to the other, lifting your rear heel off the floor and turning the hips through, along with the waist. This last drill emulates your golf finish position, mirrored on each side of the body.

Try ten repetitions of each exercise, starting on the right side. Then do another ten repetitions starting on the left side.

Figure 20: Exercise No. 3 — Empty, transfer and turn, lift the heel (right)

Figure 21: Exercise No. 3 — Empty, transfer and turn, lift the heel (left)

TRANSITION DRILL

Try this empty-handed to get a feel for the movement before practising with a club.

Go to the top of your backswing using the same feeling you generated in the **Moving the Centre** exercises, i.e. using the lower body to swing the arms. Please avoid the tendency to begin your swing with your arms and hands! At the top, hold the position for a few seconds.

If you are a right-handed golfer, check that you are sitting into the 'kwa' on your right leg and the balance point on your right foot while keeping some attention in the opposite leg and foot.

Relax your shoulders, empty your chest and pull in your navel; feel how the weight of the upper body settles down into your legs, giving you greater contact with the ground. You can now begin your transition from the ground up, transferring your weight into the left leg (for a right-handed player), once again adhering to the psoas muscle and the balance point.

Take care to turn from your waist, allowing the hips to turn just 45 degrees to the front and 45 degrees to the left. This will help you engage the t'an tien, which acts as a fulcrum of motion when applied in opposition to a stable lower body.

Drill this as a flowing motion; loosen, empty and transfer. Now try incorporating your breathing so you breathe in to the top, start your exhale as you loosen and finish breathing out while you transfer and hit through the ball.

Remember, this is a natural movement sequence and doesn't require you to think through a checklist of points, provided you are doing the Standing Meditation and moving the centre drills.

RANGE DRILLS

Here are seven unique golf drills for you to experiment with and enjoy, each based on deep, deliberate practice, which has its origins in the *bodymind* training of the East. They will help you take the emphasis off 'swing thoughts' and start the transformational process of getting in touch with what a natural golf swing actually *feels* like. It's easy to underestimate how challenging these drills are, but persevere, and you will find them an invaluable way to train for the coveted state of *relaxed readiness*, so akin to the sporting zone and flow.

DRILL NO. 1 – CHI KUNG SWING
(SWING BREATHING)

Set-up to the ball slowly, and, bringing your awareness to your t'an tien, take a few deep breaths. Loosen your shoulders, empty your chest and relax your jaw. Breathe in while you move to the top of your backswing, and then exhale all the way through to your finish position. Focus on exhaling fully as you hit through the ball, and trust your swing.

For this drill, it is essential to keep some attention on the t'an tien the whole time; otherwise, it's likely that your breathing will be in the chest, causing the upper body to lead the motion.

DRILL NO. 2 – WU CHI SWING
(POSTURE AND RELAXATION)

Working with your set-up, backswing and finish positions, aim to hold each posture for at least 30 seconds, allowing your mind and body to come together and memorise what each one feels like. Relax and breathe into your t'an tien while motionless, and make sure you're in the balance points in your feet and legs for each position.

If you adhere to the balance points for these positions, your angles of approach and impact should take care of themselves. Conversely, when you deliberately try to focus on getting your impact position right, the tendency is for the clubhead to decelerate.

When you can comfortably hold each position for 30 seconds, try for a minute, 90 seconds and so on. The emphasis should be on relaxed strength.

DRILL NO. 3 – TAI CHI SWING
(SLOW MOTION PRACTICE)

Set-up to the ball and place some attention on your feet. Swing as slowly as possible and stay relaxed throughout the motion, breathing normally. Take at least 30 seconds to complete your swing without resisting the slowness or anticipating the finish.

When you can comfortably take 30 seconds to perform your swing, try it with your eyes closed if it's safe to do so. This will really test your proprioception, which is your brain's internal map of your swing.

If working with a partner, ask them to call "Stop!" at some point during the slow motion swing. This is a great way to strengthen both your attention and your balance.

DRILL NO. 4 – A SOLID PLACE TO SWING FROM
(MAINTAINING LOWER BODY STRUCTURE)

In this drill, you will aim to maintain all the points of structure and stability in the feet and lower body while doing the slow motion swing. For instance, you will adhere to the balance points on the feet, the muscles at the tops of the legs and the hips turning just 45 degrees before the waist takes over the rotational movement. You are trying to develop the ability to keep the structure of the body in place, listening and watching for any deviations to these natural movement principles. Get them right, and they will support your technique, even under pressure.

DRILL NO. 5 – MIRROR YOUR SWING
(LEFT AND RIGHT)

In Tai Chi training, postures, empty-hand movements and weapons drills are always performed on both sides of the body to help develop a keener sense of the body in space.

This drill will also give you the ability to watch for and identify any feedback that your body is giving you, rather than letting thoughts and ideas about movement dominate. If right-handed, you'll need to get a left-handed club and so forth.

DRILL NO. 6 – PRACTISE WITH INTENTION
(IDEA, ENERGY, ACTION)

For this drill, you will practise every single shot with intensity and a clearly visualised outcome, feeling how your body responds when you take a moment to allow the idea to activate the energy within your physical being.

This is a very advanced drill, and the insights can only come if you've been practising standing and sitting quietly. Give your body a few moments to come into alignment with each intention and every picture held in your mind's eye before you start moving.

DRILL NO. 7 – UNCONDITIONAL PRACTICE SESSIONS
(FREE MOVEMENT)

Free yourself from ideas and expectations, experiment, create your own inner set-up and enjoy the feeling of allowing your body to do what it wants, unfettered by the analytical mind.

TRY THIS NO. 17
LEARNING TO LOOK

It can be useful to copy or mirror your swing coach or a player you admire, someone with the same height and body composition as you. Traditionally the Eastern arts like Tai Chi are taught by simply copying the teacher who goes through the form in front of the class without speaking. At first, due to the incessantly busy mind, it can be difficult to really look and follow. We are so preoccupied with language and the clamour for verbal instruction that we've come to believe this is the only way to learn. However, if you can stay with this exercise over a few days or weeks, it will help you to really see the overall motion of the swing, rather than giving in to the analytical mind's tendency to process a list of instructions.

TRY THIS NO. 18
DISTINGUISH HIPS FROM WAIST

Sit in a hard-backed chair with your feet on the ground and place a club across your shoulders, holding it with both palms facing forward. Keeping hold of the club, turn and look behind you. As you do this, you will naturally move from your waist while your hips remain stationary. Try to achieve this same feeling at the start of your golf swing. Even though the hips do move slightly at take-away, you'll become aware of the natural lock that starts to come into play when your hips face approximately 45 degrees away from your front line. Now your waist can take over the remainder of the rotation, adhering to the escalation of the kinetic chain, without your lower body structure starting to collapse, i.e. without the opposite femur or thigh bone and knee buckling inwards, as is usual when the hips turn too far.

TRY THIS NO. 19
ONE-LEGGED SWING

If you are a right-handed player, stand on your left leg and with the ball opposite your left foot and swing the golf club. In this posture, you'll find you have no choice about how to swing; it will all depend on your balance, flexibility and coordination. To create the intended outcome, i.e. accelerating the clubhead through the ball, the swing that emerges will be correct for your height, weight, body type etc.

When you experience what your personal swing feels like on one leg, it gives you an internal picture or proprioception map of who you really are as a golfer. You can deepen this drill with your eyes closed if it's safe to do so.

You can also progress this drill by doing one-legged standing practice; for instance, stand on your left leg and raise your right heel off the floor, or even lift the knee to waist height.

What you'll find is that to maintain your balance over several minutes, you'll need to relax your shoulders, empty your chest and focus on the body's centre of gravity.

BIBLIOGRAPHY

Bertherat, Therese and Bernstein, Carol, *The Body Has Its Reasons*, Healing Arts Press, 1989

Chuen, Lam Kam, *Chi Kung, Way of Power*, Human Kinetics, 2003

De Salzmann, Jeanne, *The Reality of Being, The Fourth Way of Gurdjieff*, Shambhala, 2011

Diepersloot, Jan, *Warriors of Stillness, Volume 1, Qigong of the Centre, Essence of Taijiquan*, 1995

Miller, Dan and Cartmell, Tim, *Xing Yi Nei Gong*, Unique Publications, 1999

Murphy, Michael, *Golf in the Kingdom*, Penguin Compass, 1997

Nicklaus, Jack, *Golf My Way*, Simon and Schuster; Revised and Updated edition, 2005

Ralston, Peter, *Cheng Hsin, The Principles of Effortless Power*, North Atlantic Books, 1989

Rosen, Steven. J, *Gita on the Green, The Mystical Tradition Behind Bagger Vance*, Continuum, 2000

Stein, Hans Joachim, *Kyudo, The Art of Zen Archery*, Element, 1988

Storey, Jayne, *Breathe Golf: The Missing Link to a Winning Performance*, Panoma Press, 2019

Yellin, Steven and Biancalana, Buddy, *The 7 Secrets of World Class Athletes*, 2010

Yeung, Sau Chung, *Practical Use of Tai Chi Chuan*, Tai Chi Co. 1976

Additional image credits:

Ensō circle image: from https://symbolsage.com/enso-symbol-and-its-meaning/

Edgar Rubin Optical Illusion on page 69: recreated by Alex Hiett

RESOURCES

OTHER BOOKS BY JAYNE STOREY AND PANOMA PRESS

Breathe Golf: The Missing Link to a Winning Performance is available online and in bookstores worldwide

THE FOLLOWING ARE AVAILABLE FROM CHI-PERFORMANCE.COM

Golf Performance Bundle (eBook, audio and video course compilation)

The Practice of High-Performance: 10 Essential Keys to Mastering Pressure (eBook and Training Guide)

12 Week Mind-Body Performance Challenge (eBook and audio programme)

Connected Putting: Harmonising Mind, Breathing and Movement on the Greens (audio programme)

Please also visit chi-performance.com and sign-up for Jayne's newsletter to receive your FREE Training Report. You will also find plenty of additional resources, including blog posts and online articles, YouTube video channels and podcasts.

FURTHER TRAINING

Jayne provides 1-2-1 and online training programmes for elite and committed amateur golfers who wish to develop a Performance Practice.

Training is also offered to coaches on an individual basis and can be facilitated as part of the PGA's Member Education Programme.

Accreditation is considered for a select number of individuals wishing to become certified trainers in the Connected Golf methods. Please get in touch via the website for more information.

Group coaching, talks and seminars are also available.

To enquire, please contact Jayne through the website.

www.chi-performance.com

ABOUT THE AUTHOR

Jayne is a Movement and Performance Coach specialising in the mind-body connection. Her expertise is based on over 30 years' training and teaching formal Buddhist meditation (Zazen) and soft-style Chinese martial arts, including Tai Chi.

Her unique approach uses simple principles of these ancient disciplines combined with traditional, deep practice to help athletes overcome anxiety, nerves and mental interference.

For almost two decades, Jayne has worked with golfers, tennis players and athletes from many other sports, helping them understand and apply this training for performing in the zone (aka *flow*).

Her experience is allied with 20 years' independent research and development of her **Chi Performance** coaching model, which provides a tried, tested and proven approach to enable the delivery of complex movement skills during high-pressure situations.

Jayne has written instructional articles for a number of sporting publications, including Golf International, Atlantic Golf & Lifestyle, Golf Monthly, National Club Golfer, Kingdom, Women's Golf Journal and Sports Coach.

In her free time, Jayne enjoys trying to speak Italian, walking, cycling, reading and learning to play classical guitar. With her lifelong interest in the martial arts, she has recently started training in Kalaripayattu, which originated in Kerala, India, and is thought to pre-date Tai Chi by several thousand years.